VARYAG

The Mysterious Journey from Ukraine to China

Ahmet Hikmet Demirayak

Varyag: The Mysterious Journey from Ukraine to China

Copyright © 2023 Ahmet Hikmet Demirayak

All rights reserved. No part of this publication may be reproduced, stored in or introduced into a retrieval system, or transmitted, in any form, or by any means (electronic, mechanical, photocopying, recording or otherwise) without the prior written permission of the author. Any person who does any unauthorised act in relation to this publication may be liable to criminal prosecution and civil claims for damages.

ISBN: 9798861757232

First Edition: November 2023

Cover Design by Murteza Albayrak
Edited by Graham Sheard

www.varyag.com

To my late father, the Public Prosecutor and Republican Senator; who never compromised from integrity.

Truth is stranger than fiction.
George Gordon Byron, Don Juan, Canto the Fourteenth, Verse 101

CONTENTS

Foreword		1
Introduction		3
1	Sixteen	7
2	Connections	19
3	Plan B	35
4	Slow Boat	57
5	Swap	69
6	The Great Game	77
7	Passage	111
8	Aircraft Carrier Style	125
Appendix - Photographs		143
Bibliography		157
Acknowledgments		161
About the Author		163

FOREWORD

There are some incidents which can only be understood as important turning points in the course of history after a certain time passes. For "history" is a series of causes and effects. Even if we know the causes, we cannot evaluate an incident's true worth until the effects come into view. The work of the esteemed Ahmet Hikmet Demirayak is a striking example of this fact.

Spread over a wide timeframe and concerning Turkey closely since 2001, when I had served as state minister of maritime affairs, "the incident of the carrier Varyag" and its passage through Turkish Straits are better assessed today – after almost a quarter of a century has passed. China obtained their first aircraft carrier when they bought Varyag via controversial methods and these methods are described thoroughly within this book. China has now produced three carriers thanks to the information Varyag provided, and China is expected to raise this number to five by 2030.

With the assistance of Varyag and consecutive aircraft carriers, China has gained the capacity to intervene at every spot in the Pacific. This has forced the US to develop new approaches, and the deck has been shuffled in the Asia-Pacific region. China's unavoidable economical rise and this new military power they have gathered will allow them to also shape the second quarter of this century.

It is undeniable that "Varyag", the subject of this very book, has played an important role in all these developments. After years of meticulous research, Ahmet Hikmet Demirayak is putting forth the incident of "Varyag", which should probably be regarded as one of the most important events of the 21st century, with all its aspects. I am of the opinion that this work, based on documents and direct witnesses, and prepared with deep sensibility, will fill an important gap in regards to a better evaluation of both past and potential developments within the region that also consists of Turkey.

Prof. Dr. Ramazan MIRZAOGLU
Turkish Maritime Affairs Minister, 1999-2002

INTRODUCTION

Nations are like people; no one wants to fall behind or be left behind. So, many countries seek to obtain technologies, particularly military ones, which they cannot design and produce within their own means. Sometimes they do this by purchasing, other times borrowing, and in some cases stealing. And some countries analyze the technologies they have obtained by different means to gain the skill to reproduce it in an improved way. This is the case with China, who have been known to replicate virtually everything… Having focused on increasing their exports and agricultural production with the reforms they initiated in the last quarter of the 20th century, managing to draw foreign investors with their low-cost and tenacious workforce, and becoming the manufacturing plant of the world, China sees nothing wrong with replicating products. In fact, these practices were encouraged by their government as recently as the 1980s. Replicating technology has simply become an important part of their industrial and social culture.

In the past, when computer piracy, devices withholding terabytes of material, or the basic processes of the internet itself – in short, the main vectors of cyberattack – did not exist, technological thievery was conducted using more old-school spying actions. (Agents who were akin to James Bond, microfilms, etc.) There were attempts to capture products themselves or their designs were attempted by illicit methods of access, which sometimes took several weeks. But what if the technological product or its design was too massive to easily smuggle or hide? Then new plans of deception were needed, and were set in motion. Just as in the case of Varyag...

The first time I heard the name "Varyag" was on a televised news report, as the name of an aircraft carrier. The report mentioned the intention to tow this engineless and rudderless carrier, purchased from Ukraine by a Chinese company, via tugs to Macau, known as the Vegas of the Far East. The carrier would be transformed into a floating entertainment center and casino. However, the Turkish government was not giving permission for Varyag's passage through Turkish Straits, whose only wayout was the Black Sea.

This fact captured my attention greatly. The research I did on the internet on the subject made me think that Varyag would not be used for recreational purposes. The company that bought the carrier from Ukraine had overlooked a small yet important matter. The carrier in question had made the headlines on the most serious newspapers and websites of the world, and many articles were written about Varyag. Therefore, this giant entertainment center (?) was getting a lot of free publicity. Nevertheless, the company neglected to trademark the domain name – varyag.com – of their twenty-million-USD carrier by paying a mere $10. Certainly, another name could have been considered for the entertainment center. However, this company was supposed to be concerned with attracting customers and tourists from around the globe. For them to fail to simply trademark their name was either a show of frivolity or an indication that their true intent was something else. Hence, I became an avid follower of the subject.

China had initiated a highly convincing, well-contemplated scheme to capture a model of aircraft carrier technology. And China achieved their goal with this setup. It had been its aim right from the beginning. Inducing a crisis between China and Turkey; causing red alarms on East Asia, especially in Taiwan, Japan and capitals of Southeast Asia; and forcing the US to review their naval policies on Asia-Pacific region, the story of Varyag saw some facts disclosed in time, but some others were

INTRODUCTION

admitted tacitly from remaining silent. But there are also some facts that have not and cannot be disclosed in this long and sometimes chaotic tale.

I did not content myself with the spare facts presented by global media, and spent long years scrutinising them and doing research on the issue that sometimes felt as if it would never end. I questioned every bit of information from every source I could find to ensure its accuracy. On the other hand, twenty-two years have passed, waiting for the consequences of Varyag's tale to emerge and, as the Turkish phrase goes, the subject has become well-steeped. As the owner of "varyag.com", the time has come to reveal the known, the unknown and, most importantly, the misknown.

CHAPTER 1

SIXTEEN

Stepping into the third millennia, we thought that many things would change. We thought this because twentieth century science fiction, on the whole, had described the 2000s as an era of substantial developments for humanity. We still expected various issues, but we thought they would occur in a more prosperous, peaceful, and calm era...

This was indeed our expectation for the new millennium. At the time, every person with access to a microphone would suggest that we were on the verge of great things, and it was strongly felt that profound technological transformation would pave the way for developments in many fields —from medicine to agriculture, and from tackling environmental issues to the exploration of space. Everyone expected great things. But was it really everyone? That does not seem to be true. On the eve of this brand-new millennium, some people wanted different things —some people in China, for instance.

China Information News, the media outlet of the National Bureau of Statistics of China, published a story on January 14, 2002. The statistics displayed a 4,200-participant-survey, which was conducted in November 2001, just at the beginning of the millennium, in different Chinese cities. What makes this survey relevant is that when the participants were asked, "What do you expect from the next five years?", 23.2% of them replied, "China must build its first aircraft carrier." This reply was 16th on the list of answers.

It was a rather interesting outcome. Generalizing from the survey results, roughly one-fourth of Chinese people wanted an aircraft carrier for their own country rather than things that would directly upgrade their living standards. Humanistic expectations and vital services were cast aside, and for some the carrier was regarded as a greater necessity.

However, why would Chinese people, despite risking objections from many people of the civilized world, desire a national carrier above public service? By what measurement was the aircraft carrier more important than humanistic needs that could bring greater prosperity? It would not be possible to answer this without taking a look at the history of China.

In Chinese history, there is a period between the First Opium War of 1839, and the end of WWII in 1945. Some call it the Century of Humiliation (Bainian guochi). In this era, China was attacked by Western imperialist powers and Japan, lost her sovereignty, and went through a massive domestic disintegration. This era had brought China to the verge of losing her national unity altogether.

The decadence and failure of the Qing Dynasty, which had been ruling China since 1644, against foreign attacks, incited the Chinese Revolution of 1911. This brought the two-thousand-year era of imperial rule to an end. The Chinese Republic that replaced it achieved only partial domination, and this paved the way for many subsequent upheavals. In 1927, the Chinese Civil War erupted between nationalists and communists. These were domestic struggles with large casualties that temporarily subsided in 1937 when Japan declared that it was against China, allowing two opposing stances to collaborate temporarily against a common enemy.

The Second Sino-Japanese War saw Japan's occupation of the majority of Eastern China. This occupation lasted until Japan surrendered at the end of WWII in 1945. After the Japanese threat was eliminated, the civil war was rekindled. Ultimately, the Chinese Communist Party (CCP), led by Mao Zedong, seized power, and declared the foundation of the

People's Republic of China. Members of the Chinese National Party, led by Chiang Kai-shek, withdrew to Taiwan, and declared independence, claiming that the continued existence of "The Republic of China", founded in 1912 as a larger sovereign state, was retained in this island.

"The Century of Humiliation" contained many tragic episodes for Chinese people, but one of them—at least as an explanation for the carrier demand—stands out. During the Sino-French War of 1883-1885, one of the most tragic defeats in the Chinese military history took place. The Fujian Fleet of the Chinese Navy included eleven ironclad warships, but on August 23, 1884, it was destroyed by the French in less than an hour! China has never forgotten this.

In much more recent events, the Taiwan Strait Crisis and the bombing of the Chinese Embassy in Belgrade in the 1990s are examples of why some in China feel they must possess carriers as a deterring force and a means of intervention in potential issues when necessary.

The Taiwan Strait Crisis broke out in 1996. February and March of that year saw China's missile tests and military manoeuvres against Taiwan, the country which China incessantly claims as her own, turn into an international crisis. The "Superpower" US was not expected to display indifference. However, the Clinton administration was quick to position two aircraft carrier battle groups near Taiwan.

Taiwan, the place that General Douglas MacArthur, a significant figure in American history who commanded on the Pacific Front in WWII, branded as "unsinkable aircraft carrier" had a vital importance for US interest in the region. The US was browbeating China by sending gigantic warships and, in a sense, telling her to "pull it together."

Meanwhile, the Taiwanese in Taipei organized an amity parade in front of the American Institute, the unofficial American embassy, with a "Welcome" banner for one of the carriers, USS Independence. China found it impossible to withstand this power, and once again, so to speak, had to take a deep breath and swallow.

The bombing of the Chinese Embassy in Belgrade occurred on May 7, 1999. The event brought China and the US face to face once more. During the NATO operation in Yugoslavia, missiles launched by US warplanes hit the Chinese Embassy in Belgrade. The incident, which ended the lives of three Chinese journalists, sparked great outrage in China. US President Clinton stated that the Yugoslav Federal Directorate for Supply and Procurement near the embassy was targeted and done in error. This explanation was not received well by Chinese people.

Only a few hours after the bombing, a former member of the Chinese People's Liberation Army (PLA) messaged in the chat room of a minor website in the Henan province, calling for the construction of China's first aircraft carrier. Even in those years when the internet was not yet quite widespread, this message from a local website went viral shortly and lit the fuse of a popular campaign.

Only three days after the bombing, the newspaper Henan Youth Daily published a special edition to promote a donation campaign for the launch of a specific fund for the construction of aircraft carriers. This appeal created a tremendous impression in no time. Henan Commercial Daily, Central Construction News, and Sanmenxia Daily also published similar editions afterward.

The public showed massive interest in the media campaign as well. Meanwhile, the organizers obtained promises for 11 million Renminbi of donations from more than ten organizations and thousands of people. Thus, the first step was taken to make this Chinese dream come true.

To paraphrase "The North Remembers!" from the popular show of recent years, "Game of Thrones", we can say, "China had remembered." "The Century of Humiliation" was still fresh in public memory. A mere forage of the ashes had been more than enough for the fire to blaze again.

SIXTEEN

Certainly, the matter has a military-political aspect to it, besides Chinese nationalism. A strong navy would be of great importance for the Chinese government to demonstrate its strength and look after its interests against foreign powers. As is known, China is one of the five permanent members of the United Nations Security Council. When the 2000s came, which country among the council members was the only one lacking an aircraft carrier group? Your guess is correct: the People's Republic of China.

In those years, China was not the only country that did not have a carrier, but the giant of the East was not content with this. The Chinese military, the People's Liberation Army Navy (PLAN), considered carriers part of their wish for a stronger blue-water navy, which would operate in the farthest parts of the ocean. But it was also considered to have symbolic value, as a kind of metaphorical blue diamond or Heart of Ocean.

To make this dream come true, China had developed an aircraft carrier research and development programme. According to Admiral Liu Huaqing, who is seen as the father of the modern Chinese Navy and a strong advocate of this programme, Chinese naval doctrine has to take two phases. First, PLAN should preserve the security of Chinese territorial waters. Second, China should have a blue-water navy that reflects her strength. Hence, with the process in which Liu Huaqing served as PLAN commander in 1982-1988, and as Vice Chairman of the Central Military Commission in 1989-1997, the Chinese aircraft carrier programme made solid progress.

At this point, we ought not to overlook these sentences by Zhang Zhaozhong, a military theoretician of National Defense University of People's Liberation Army, that were published in 1996 by Ordnance Knowledge, a Ukrainian military publication:

"We need to increase our knowledge of ship construction. Purchasing seems to be the only way for emerging nations to develop aircraft carriers."

Zhang Zhaozhong had a reputation as a soldier with rear admiral rank in PLAN and frequent commentaries on state TV. Aside from his pinpoint estimations regarding The Gulf War, he made inaccurate predictions for the Iraq War. Zhaozhong is also known for his critical remarks, which veil China's true military strength.

Even if this expert theoretician is occasionally mistaken, between 1985-1998 China procured three out-of-service and one incomplete aircraft carriers by unofficial means. The route indicated by this expert figure was virtually China's route.

China was determined not to remain as the only permanent member of the United Nations Security Council that did not possess an aircraft carrier group.

The first aircraft carrier procured by unofficial means is HMAS Melbourne, which was received in 1985 by a Chinese ship dismantling company from Australia, with all electronic and weaponry systems disabled. The Chinese company paid 1.4 million Australian dollars (1.1 million USD) for the carrier, which had served between 1955 and 1982 before she was scrapped. As might be expected, the carrier was not dismantled immediately but analysed by navy engineers within the aircraft carrier development programme.

After Melbourne, two Kiev class carriers were bought. They were from the same manufacturing line, so they were "sister ships", and they were named Kiev and Minsk.

Four Kiev class carriers were constructed by the former Soviet Union in the 1970s and 80s. These were Kiev, Minsk, Novorossiyks and Baku; all served in Soviet and post-Soviet Russian navies. They were equipped with warship weaponry with their unorthodox designs, including missile and torpedo systems on the foredeck. Each had a flight deck on their portside that supported both vertically landing and departing jets and helicopters. Branded also as "cruisers carrier" for these specialties, these carriers were active until the mid-90s. Baku was renamed Admiral Gorshkov in the Russian Navy, went out

SIXTEEN

of service in 1996, and following a thorough revision, sold in 2010 to India for 2.35 billion dollars.

Kiev, the first of the two Russian carriers China bought, had retired after serving between 1975 and 1993. In 1996, a Chinese company of Tianjin origin bought Kiev. After being exhibited as a piece of Binhai Military Theme Park until 2004, the carrier was transformed in 2011 into a luxury hotel, which cost roughly 15.6 million USD.

On the other hand, Minsk arrived in China in a slightly indirect manner. She was first bought by a South Korean company in 1995 as scrap, along with Novorossiysk. In 1997, this South Korean company dismantled Novorossiysk, which had previously been out of service due to a severe fire in the engine room. Minsk, having served between 1978 and 1993, was retired for an undisclosed accident. Then, it was bought under the condition that it would be used for other than military purposes. It was purchased by the Shenzhen Minsk Aircraft Carrier Industry, a Chinese company, for 5 million USD and made its way toward China.

Without an engine, weaponry, or electronic equipment, Minsk was sent into Guangdong province to become a museum. As of 2000, she began to serve in a military theme park in Shenzhen city of the Yantian province, as "Minsk World", and in this process, the former carrier changed hands due to various reasons, such as bankruptcy and mere sell-outs.

Even after buying these three militarily non-functional aircraft carriers and inspecting them, China was still far from reaching her main target. However, a fourth carrier would change things considerably, bought in an adventurous way, and, of course, unofficially again. The fourth carrier China bought unofficially via private companies was Varyag: an incomplete, Kuznetsov class, Soviet product. The Kuznetsov class, with an advanced design comparable to the Kiev class, had ski-jumps. This feature enabled high-performing traditional planes to depart with their own engine power and arrestor wires for smoother landings. Admiral Kuznetsov, first of the class, was put in dry dock in 1982, to be completed in eight years. The second and the last of the class, Varyag, began its construction in 1985.

Actually, the name Varyag was inspired by Scandinavian sailors that existed in ninth century Russia. However, the first name under consideration was "Riga." This is because there was a tradition in the Soviet Navy to name aircraft carriers with the names of capitals of autonomous republics under the influence of the Soviet Union. Upon the rise of anti-Soviet sentiment in Baltic nations towards the end of the 1980s, the name Riga, Latvia's capital, was discarded to be replaced by "Varyag." However, she was not the first ship to be named Varyag in Russian naval history. Previously, in 1904, a Russian warship with the same name had been cornered in Korean waters and forced to surrender. After refusing to comply and receiving fatal wounds, the commander Rudnev and his crew sank their ship to prevent Japanese capture. But why was this Varyag, with a name of historical legacy, an incomplete carrier?

Incomplete Varyag, on the left, and Admiral Kuznetsov at Chernomorsky Shipyard. *Mykolaiv, 1989.*

SIXTEEN

Upon the disintegration of the Soviet Union in 1991, the ownership of the carrier was transferred to a newly independent Ukraine. As of 1992, she was mostly completed – about 70%. Despite this fact, Ukraine halted the construction of the carrier. This decision had an entirely economical basis.

The carrier's total cost was 2.4 billion USD, and more than 500 million USD was needed to complete it. In brief, Varyag was an economic liability for Ukraine, who was struggling to become self-reliant. When the construction was halted in 1992, the Chinese government negotiated with Ukrainian counterparts to purchase Varyag as an aircraft carrier, but it led to no conclusions. In fact, the Ukrainian government even denied the occurrence of the negotiations.

There was a name on the Chinese side who, upon the failure of the negotiations, wanted the matter to be closed once and for all: Jiang Zemin, who served as General Secretary of the Communist Party of China and Chairman of the Central Military Commission, simultaneously holding the Presidency of People's Republic of China to become the supreme leader of the country.

President Jiang Zemin's judgment would not change until the mid-2000. However, there was something even the President did not know: The project to bring Varyag into PLAN had been initiated in 1996. So how indeed had it begun without even his knowing?

Varyag, the rudderless and engineless carrier, was bought from Ukraine in 1998 by Chong Lot Travel Agency, a Macau company. Chong Lot declared the reason for purchase as positioning the carrier into Macau – a Portuguese colony then – and transforming it into an entertainment center and casino.

When the purchase of Varyag was put on hold, the media of Hong Kong – which had been handed over from the UK to China only one year previously – refused to keep silent and claimed that Chong Lot was acting on behalf of the Chinese government. The Chinese Embassy in Kiev rejected this allegation. However, the damage was done. The case for

VARYAG

Varyag had long ceased to be a domestic business of China and became a matter of global interest.

Varyag received widespread media attention worldwide. International networks such as BBC, CNN, and NBC broadcast several stories about her, and the West was all but alarmed about her.

Also, one aspect of the matter concerned Turkey: Varyag had to cross the Turkish Straits to arrive at China. However, Turkey was not allowing it. It was felt that this giant carrier would compromise the settlements on the Bosphorus (Istanbul Strait) and the security of sea traffic.

BBC broadcast a story with the title "Aircraft carrier 'trapped' in the Black Sea." This story featured Joop Timmermans' remarks. Timmermans was the CEO of Dutch ocean towage, salvage and offshore company ITC, of which one of their tugs had towed the carrier in circles in the Black Sea outside of Turkish territorial waters. He stated that "[They] believe it is a political issue converted into a technical issue... apparently there are people who do not like to see China having another aircraft carrier."

A Washington Post article by John Ward Anderson summarized the uncertainty in the Western world remarkably well: "Chinese investors see the Varyag as a floating casino and luxury hotel. To some Western military analysts, it's a potentially lethal, 67,000-ton supercarrier. For many impartial observers, it's a rusted hunk of junk…"

The Australian newspaper ARN's article "Soviet warship, no engine, seeks future in entertainment" stated, "The boldest gamblers might bet on the future of the Varyag," to underline the obscurity of the giant carrier's future.

In the end, the winners were those who had bet on military analysts. Because Varyag (or Liaoning, with its new name) is today serving the Chinese People's Liberation Army Navy as the first aircraft carrier of the country. The Chinese state has made PLAN's blue-water navy dream come true and satisfied the public's expectations, crowning this victory by giving the carrier bow number "Sixteen."

Then, how on earth is Varyag, which was objected even by her own head of state, and blocked by Turkey, used as an aircraft carrier today?

The answer to this lies in the mysterious transoceanic story of Varyag's epic journey from Mykolaiv, Ukraine, swinging by Macau, Hong Kong, USA, and Turkey, before reaching Dalian.

CHAPTER 2

CONNECTIONS

Before glancing at Varyag's movie-like journey, it is worth giving an eye to Macau, the center of the whole story.

Located on the edge of the Southern China Sea, upon Pearl River Delta, Macau is a former Portuguese colony. The 12.7-square-mile land area resides 23 miles southwest of Hong Kong, comprising Macau Peninsula and the islands of Taipa and Coloane.

The first known residents of the region were Fujianese fishers and Guangdongese farmers. Having limited settlement until the last quarter of the thirteenth century, Macau became a cramped zone when members of the Southern Song Dynasty and their nearly fifty thousand followers took refuge here to escape from the 1277 Mongolian invasion. The region attracted fishers from all over the southern coast of China for the next three hundred years.

In this era, Hoklo boat people, who earned their livelihood with their boats, began to use Macau as a trading center. This was due to the region's increased population and its location on the mouth of Pearl River. However, Macau did not develop into a residential area until the sixteenth century, when Portuguese merchants arrived at A Ma Gao [A Ma's Place]. The name Macau is considered to be coined from the A Ma Temple, which was built on the entrance of the sheltered inner port, in honour of Goddess A Ma's, the patron of mariners and fishers.

As of 1557, the Portuguese had rented Macau from the Ming Dynasty (1368-1644) of China. They used Macau as a trading center and made her the first European colony in Eastern Asia. Macau was mainly administered by Portuguese. However, she operated under Chinese dominance between 1557 and 1887. In 1644, upon the fall of the Ming Dynasty, the Qing Dynasty, of Manchu origin, rose to power, but the change had little to no effect on the Portuguese settlement in Macau. After China lost the Opium Wars to Western countries, Portugal ceased to pay rental fees and taxes and seized first Taipa, then Coloane islands, in 1851 and 1864, respectively. With the Manchu-Portugal agreement of 1887, Portugal was granted indefinite control and administration rights on Macau under the condition that she would not be handed over to any third parties without China's permission.

Retaining its colony status for a long time, Macau became the only neutral port in Southern China after the Japanese invaded Guangzhou and Hong Kong in WWII. This neutrality caused thousands of refugees fleeing away from the horrors of the war to rush into Macau. As a result, the region's population of 200,000 more than tripled over a few years to 700,000. After the end of the war, when the PRC was founded in 1949, many refugees and the supporters of the Chinese Nationalist Party, known as Kuomintang, also fled to Macau.

After the bloodless Carnation Revolution of 1974, when the Salazar dictatorship gave way to democracy, Portugal tried to restore Macau to Chinese domination. However, at that time, China's attention was focused on diplomatically settling Hong Kong's future. They had abandoned the city after the First Opium War to become a colony of the British Empire. Thus, taking Macau back was postponed indefinitely.

The proceedings regarding Macau commenced one year after the Sino-British Joint Declaration of 1984, by which the restoration of Hong Kong to China was agreed to take place in 1997. After two years of negotiation, the Sino-Portuguese Joint Declaration of 1987 secured Macau's transfer to China, which was completed on December 20, 1999. In line with China's

CONNECTIONS

"one country, two systems" principle, Macau became another Special Administrative Region after the fashion of Hong Kong.

This is Macau's eight hundred years of history told in a nutshell. Today she is described as "the Monte Carlo of the East, the biggest entertainment center of Asia where casinos and sex tourism is most common."

On the Chinese mainland, gambling was officially outlawed after the Communist Party's rise. Gambling is also prohibited in Hong Kong except for horse-racing bets. Hence, Macau is the only region in China to allow gambling.

This liberty dates back to the 1850s, when the Portuguese government legalized gambling for extra income.

The monopolizing of Macanese gambling started in 1930 when the company Hou Heng was granted the privilege to operate on all of the allowed types of gambling. In 1937, the Portuguese government issued a decree to integrate the administration of different games, and the monopoly privilege was handed over to the company Tai Heng. This corporation introduced the card game Baccarat to Macau, but on December 31st, 1961, it lost its gambling privileges as administration was deregulated, and bids for new administration were invited in 1962.

There were two bidding companies: One of them was already operating in the market, Tai Heng; and the other was Sociedade de Turismo e Diversões de Macau (STDM), also formed that year by Hong Kongese and Macanese businesspeople Stanley Ho (Ho Hung Sun / He Hongsen), and their associates Teddy Yip, Yip Hon, and Henry Fok.

In the end, the new company won the tender. STDM brought millions of gamblers here, by introducing Western games and modernizing sea transportation between Macau and Hong Kong. It would not be an exaggeration to claim that STDM represented a tipping point for Macau, and the gambling industry broke through after 1962. In 1986, the Legislative Assembly of Macau put the law, which limited the allowed license count to three, into force. However, this was not implemented in practice. The license obtained by STDM was extended in 1986 for another fifteen years, and the other two possible licenses were not granted to any other companies.

Since Macau was a candidate to become the world's gambling capital, it is not quite surprising that the setup in which Chong Lot purchased Varyag to transform her into a floating casino in Macau was taken seriously by international intelligence services. We should admit that Project Varyag was indeed a brilliantly planned setup.

At this point, both the company, which was founded in Macau to purchase Varyag, and its founder should be taken under scrutiny. It is rather significant that such a small company planned to purchase an aircraft carrier that could not be deemed economical within its standard budget.

As already indicated in the first chapter, the negotiations with Ukraine for the purchase of Varyag got stuck initially. Therefore, the head of state of China had decided to walk away from the project. President Jiang Zemin informed the government about the decision to make it official. All of the top executives were aware of this. However, Ukrainian President Leonid Kuchma's visit to Beijing in December 1995, as the official guest of President Jiang Zemin, would change certain things. After the visit, Ukrainian Vice Prime Minister Anatoliy Kinakh, who had accompanied Kuchma in China, stated in his interview with the Interfax-Ukraine news agency that many options were debated during the negotiations, including Varyag's completion in one of the Chinese shipyards as well as selling her off as scrap metal. Most significant among Kinakh's words was that Varyag's selling as an aircraft carrier had been one of the possibilities. Although offer-bringing Ukraine was hopeful of the negotiations, a change of heart did not seem possible for President Jiang Zemin. However, Ukraine's "Buy her any old way!" approach had still drawn particular attention. High-ranked officers of the army – especially naval officers – regarded Varyag as too good a deal to let go. Considering that the head of state might change his decision, they elected to find some party to purchase the carrier commercially and acted upon this unofficially.

The officers contacted various millionaire businesspeople to convince them for Varyag, but they were rejected on every attempt. No one wanted to invest with ambiguous objectives and for unknown ends.

Despite all these refusals of businesspeople, the undaunted officers at last visited Chinluck Holding Company Limited, which operated in commerce, catering, culture, entertainment, and real estate industries in Hong Kong. The man who would materialize their secret project was standing before them: Xu Zengping, also known as Cheng Zhen Shu, former basketball star of Chinese People's Liberation Army! But who was this man actually?

Xu Zengping joined the PLA in 1971 in Jinan, the capital of the Shandong province of China. He was then posted to Guangzhou, the capital, and the biggest city of Guangdong province, in the sports department. With his 6'1'' height, he played for and captained the military team for a dozen years, before his discharge in 1983. Afterward, he stayed in the province and established a farming and carpet trading company. In due course, he expanded his business and moved to Hong Kong with his wife in 1988, establishing Chinluck Holding Company on April 4, 1991.

In Minnie Chan's interview, "Unlucky guy tasked with buying China's aircraft carrier," which was published on April 29, 2015, in the South China Morning Post, Xu Zengping claimed that the officers who reached out to him in 1996 had met, instead of many millionaires, only two Hong Kongese businessman of wealth, with himself being the third. The officers who had put their names behind the project were He Pengfei, then Vice-Admiral of PLAN, and Major General Ji Shengde, the military intelligence director.

Again, according to Xu, the symbolic face of the Project Varyag and the one who persuaded him was He Pengfei: A soldier who was promoted into lieutenant general rank in 1994.

Ji Shengde was Ji Pengfei's son; his father was the foreign minister in 1972, when Nixon visited China. However, Xu attested that the real master behind the plan was Ji Shengde. In fact, along with Ji, many officers, with their patriotism and their passion for the army, had conducted preliminary studies for the acquisition of the carrier.

Regarding his statements in the interview, Xu and He had a series of negotiations between April 1996 and February 1998. These took place in remote places, such as pathways, when the plan's details had to be debated.

The most unforgettable was the one on July 10, 1996. This meeting had taken place during the ceremony for the North Sea Fleet's first visit to North Korea, in the city Qingdao of Shandong province. This was highly exceptional because a civilian was seldom invited to such a ceremony.

After the event, He wanted Xu to stay at Beihai Hotel, property of the navy, for three days. This would provide enough time to convince Xu. The last of these days, He and Xu took a navy flight to Beijing, debating all along the trip. In the end, Xu said he would think about going to Ukraine to negotiate the purchase. Finally, in March 1997, Xu gambled with the greatest bet of his life and accepted He's offer. The two figures carried on with their regular meetings until late 1998.

Xu refrained from naming soldiers in the interview, "Mission Impossible," published on January 19, 2015. The soldiers had warned Xu about two points: the navy would not support this financially, and Beijing was not encouraging the project. If he accepted the deal under these circumstances, Xu would be challenging the national policy.

Xu explained to SCMP his decision to agree in the face of all the obstacles: "I was chosen as the person to purchase the aircraft carrier. I had realized this was an impossible mission because an act such as purchasing a carrier was not a business of a company or an individual. It was state business, but my passion forced me into it. For this business was a 'now or never' type of chance for China." With these statements, Xu referred to the movie Mission Impossible, virtually ensuring the interview title.

Some of the developments after Xu's acceptance could be found in an interview of April 2015. According to his own words, Xu had first used loans for the necessary amount. Then, as collateral, he provided the 41.800-square-meter land area of Peng Chau, the tiny island to the northeast of Hong Kong's Lantau Island. However, this business was greater than that, and the loan was not sufficient. Therefore, he borrowed 230 million Chinese yuan (approximately 27.77 million USD) from a Hong Kongese business associate without any guarantees or collateral and further sold his house on Hong Kong Peak. All of this was not easy, as Xu was venturing into this business during the peak of the Asian financial crisis.

To carry out the project, he had opened two offices, in April 1997 in Beijing and in Kiev two months later. The Beijing office was there to rent three business suites in the Grand Hotel to give instructions to Ukrainian experts. The management of this office was entrusted with Xiao Yun, late general Xiao Hua's son, a member of the Central Committee of the Communist Party of China, who had retired from his post of vice presidency of naval air force armaments department. The person who came to terms with him was Ji Shengde, or, with Xu's words, "the real master."

In the Kiev office, a dozen naval and ship construction experts were posted to ascertain the carrier's condition and the requests of Ukrainian officials. These experts had previously worked for China State Shipbuilding Company and Commission for Science, Technology, and Industry for National Defense; and also took part in the delegation that Beijing sent to Ukraine in 1992 to inspect the prospect of the Varyag purchase.

During the negotiations, the experts said that the Ukrainian shipbuilder did not want Varyag to be used for military purposes. Thus, as they were enjoined beforehand, they claimed that the carrier would be transformed into a tremendous floating hotel and casino. To endorse this, Xu founded Chong Lot, his shell corporation in August 1997 and spent 6 million Hong Kong dollars (775 thousand USD) to obtain the necessary paperwork to open the casino.

The Beijing Office was closed after the agreement with Ukrainians. However, the Ukraine Office remained open until July 1999, when Varyag left Black Sea Shipyard. Ultimately, Xu's narration corresponds to this. Because the other actors of the story, the soldiers, never spoke, as they were never allowed to speak. Likewise, neither He nor Ji, the names Xu claimed as the backroom figures of the project, were in for a satisfying end to their stories.

He Pengfei suffered a heart attack in March 2001 and died at the age of 56. Ji Shengde was dismissed from his duties in June 1999, after the Lai Changxing smuggling scandal. In 2000 he was sentenced to capital punishment, but the execution was postponed for two years. With his good behavior in this process, the sentence was reduced to twenty years in prison, which he is still serving.

In all that he reveals, Xu's scrupulous reservation about two matters catches attention. The first is the identity of Project Varyag's real founder. Were the project executives He and Ji, or could the real architect be Admiral Liu Huaqing, the father of the modern Chinese navy, who maintained that China should have her own aircraft carrier?

Secondly, in his interviews, Xu never mentioned what happened in Macau or the founding days of Chong Lot. Therefore, it is worth taking a closer look at those two matters.

The sudden appearance of the name Admiral Liu Huaqing should not bemuse anyone. After all, this story is full of surprises. Xu, knowingly or not, never expressed Liu Huaqing's role in the secret project; but since the company, via which he got a loan by collateralizing his land, was exposed in the assets and liabilities lawsuit, it is possible to carry the Admiral's name to the top of the Project Varyag.

Registered in Hong Kong, this company was run by Lieutenant Colonel Liu Chaoying, daughter of Admiral Liu Huaqing. Liu Chaoying was also a senior executive of China Aerospace International Holding Limited (CASIL). This was a branch of China Aerospace Science and Technology Corporation, the state-owned satellite development company of the 1990s.

This situation would not be confusing for those who know China intimately. Nepotism is quite common in this country. Hence, the older the top senior executives of the Chinese Communist Party and the Chinese People's Liberation Army's military leaders get, the more critical roles their sons and daughters undertake. These privileged kids, known as princelings in China, while already taking ranks in the party, are also key players in the business world. That is why it is no wonder that princelings Ji Shengde and Liu Chaoying, have crossed paths with each other. As you might have guessed, it was Ji Shengde who made Xu get in touch with Lieutenant Colonel Liu Chaoying.

Now, as to the second matter: Why was Xu omitting Macau? What had happened there?

It is a well-known fact that all the casinos in Macau had been monopolized by Stanley Ho's company, STDM, since 1962, and he had come up with a special franchising system for gambling. Also, since Macau casinos had become a magnet for local and Hong Kongese triads (Chinese mafia), the underworld had slowly and silently penetrated casinos.

As the government of Macau and Stanley Ho failed to preserve the balance of power in the underworld and Macau's transfer to China came to a close, triad wars had reached a peak. Given the circumstances, it is not hard to guess that a Hong Kongese of Chinese origin would not have the luxury to waltz into Macau without any backup powers and say, "I want to establish a company with the aim of opening a casino."

So, how could this be possible? It was possible because the critical figure of the Project Varyag, Ji Shengde, was the intelligence director and thus, had the power and connections to have an important role here. Through Ji's connections in Macau, Ng Lap Seng, and Chan Kai-kit (Chio Ho-cheong), Xu was able to move freely in Macau. Thus, he found the shell corporation which would purchase the carrier.

Ng Lap Seng, born in 1948, is said to have come to Macau from the Nanhai region of Guangdong province by bribing the border police. Despite arriving at Macau with few properties, then prospering and getting international attention in the 1990s, Ng Lap Seng was regarded as a "low profile businessman." Later, he owned the Hotel Fortuna.

An old-style place, Hotel Fortuna included a nightclub in which karaoke rooms were provided with lap dancers. There were also massage salons with exotic female hostesses from Europe, Asia, and Russia. This hotel, with limited interest from locals, had a very special customer portfolio which made it very important: Mafia, local gangs and most importantly, high-ranked officers of the People's Liberation Army!

The nightclub of the Hotel Fortuna was frequented by senior soldiers. The soldiers would get free rooms and à la carte services. The pains taken for PLA members provided Ng significant connections among top-ranked soldiers.

As for Chan Kai-kit, he was a Thailand-born Hainanese and a prominent businessman and politician of Macau. He had won the legislative assembly election in 1996 with the triad 14K's help, which was the world's second-largest triad with 20,000 members.

Being no ordinary businessman, Chan Kai-kit was running the restaurant "No Hands" in Macau. No Hands was where female waitresses would feed the customers barehanded to free the customers' hands for various activities. Chan's wife, Chan Yik Zee Elsie, had won the Miss Peace prize in 1986 Miss Asia. Throughout their married life, Elsie provided Thai women with several entertainment centers in Macau.

This process, explained with details, shows that the meetings between these two connections Ji provided and Xu –

possibly also attended by Ji – had taken place at Ng's Fortuna Hotel to stay under the radar.

These meetings in Hotel Fortuna bore fruit in time. Thanks to Chan Kai-kit's political might, as of August 11, 1997, the founding contract of the tourism company Agência Turística e Diversões Chong Lot (Chong Lot Tourist and Amusement Agency Limited) was signed in the presence of Notary Alexandre Correia da Silva.

BOLETIM OFICIAL DE MACAU — II SÉRIE	N.º 34 — 20-8-1997
CARTÓRIO PRIVADO MACAU	Artigo quarto
CERTIFICADO	O capital social, integralmente subscrito e realizado em dinheiro, é de um milhão de patacas, equivalentes a cinco milhões de escudos, ao câmbio de cinco escudos por pataca, nos termos do Decreto-Lei número trinta e três barra setenta e sete barra M, de vinte de Agosto, e corresponde à soma das seguintes quotas:
Agência Turística e Diversões Chong Lot, Limitada	
Certifico, para efeitos de publicação, que, por escritura de 11 de Agosto de 1997, lavrada a fls. 45 e seguintes do livro de notas para escrituras diversas n.º 18-C, deste Cartório, foi constituída uma sociedade por quotas de responsabilidade limitada, denominada «Agência Turística e Diversões Chong Lot, Limitada», nos termos dos artigos em anexo:	a) Cheng, Zhen Shu, uma quota no valor de novecentas e oitenta mil patacas; e b) Chong, Lap Cheung, uma quota no valor de vinte mil patacas.
	Artigo quinto

The founding contract of the Chong Lot Travel Agency. *Official Bulletin of Macau.*

With a primary foundational purpose of management, tourism, and entertainment industries foremost, the total paid-up capital of the company was 125 thousand USD. 98% of the company capital belonged to Cheng, Zhen Shu (Xu Zengping), and 2% was Chong, Lap Cheung's. The company was located in the center of Macau, at Avenida da Praia Grande 335, on the fourth floor. According to Western media, there was no door numbered 335. Which means the company was founded at a non-existent address. However, this point remained obscure too. Because Xu had lost the majority of the company's shares, he founded in 1999. That is why he avoided the name Macau meticulously in his interviews. Now, let us get back to Varyag.

After founding a company that would purchase the carrier as a casino, it came to get Stanley Ho's approval, monopolizing gambling in Macau. Ji Shengde, taking Ng Lap Seng along, would have talked to Stanley Ho in person. Ng Lap Seng also owned a small trade center, which linked his Fortuna Hotel to Stanley Ho's Lisboa Casino. Moreover, Stanley Ho and Ng Lap Seng were also partners in Nam Van Lakes Project.

It is worth talking about Stanley Ho, one of the richest men in Asia, known as the "King of Gambling." Stanley Ho was born in 1921, in one of the richest and most powerful clans of Hong Kong, the Ho Tung family. When he was just thirteen, his father went bankrupt during the Great Depression, and Ho left his family to flee to Vietnam. After getting a scholarship at Hong Kong University, Ho had to leave his education with the outbreak of WWII. Upon the Japanese invasion of Hong Kong, he waded into the refugees from the Chinese mainland and took a boat to Macau. His first fortune came during the war, with Macau's smuggling of luxury goods to the Chinese border. After founding a kerosene company in 1943, he used his profits to found a building company.

In 1948, Stanley Ho married Clementina Leitao, daughter of a reputed lawyer with links to Portuguese high society. Ho and associates' efforts to win these connections and Macanese executives' favour supposedly have come in useful for their gaining the gambling monopoly.

Before Macau went back into the Chinese administration in 1999, there were many debates and studies regarding the liberation of the gambling industry from different perspectives. The forty-year-old casino monopoly concession, which Stanley Ho held, would end as of 2001. Facing a threat of losing his license, Ho was not content with this. The meeting between the King of Casinos and the PLA general and his permission to Varyag's existence in Macau could be seen as a part of the licensing bargain.

The project was presented to Stanley Ho in his favour. Xu's Chong Lot would buy a scrap aircraft carrier, which shipbuilding experts would then inspect to be brought into Macau. This carrier would be transformed into a grand casino and an entertainment center with a hotel, and the management would be left to Stanley Ho.

The presented project included a multi-functioning entertainment center with a hotel of 600 rooms, a casino, a disco, restaurants, and nightclubs. Also, a new name was coined for Varyag: Ocean Entertainment Center. In fact, during a press conference in Hong Kong in November 1998, Xu Zengping expressed these proposals as features of the project.

It is possible that Stanley Ho accepted the offer with the dream of getting the license once more and running a giant floating casino. And in fact, about the license, his worst fears did not come true. In 2001, Macau Special Administrative Region decided to grant three gambling licenses to bring new dynamics to the gambling industry and build a solid basis for the business progress. The tender of the same year had 21 offers in total, from Macau, Hong Kong, the United States of America, the United Kingdom, Malaysia, Australia, and Taiwan. On February 8, 2002, Macau SAR declared the tender results. Sociedade de Jogos de Macau (SJM), a subsidiary of STDM, was among the winners.

However, as one would guess, Varyag never arrived in Macau after her purchase. This giant carrier passed Macau to be towed into Dalian Port on China's Liaoning province. It is not quite challenging to imagine the massive disappointment Stanley Ho must have felt. To amend this, in 2006, Ho got a draft from internationally reputed French architect Paul Andreu which resembled Varyag's hull. The project, named Oceanus by Ho per se, which was expected to cost him 800 million USD was a multi-functional entertainment center that included a hotel of 600 rooms, a casino, a movie theatre, stores, and flats. Oceanus would be built on the port next to the Macau-Hong Kong ferry pier to symbolize a naval change for Macau.

Apparently, Stanley Ho had come to terms with having been a part of a transoceanic fraud and decided to at least have a non-floating entertainment center. Unfortunately, the Project Oceanus never came to pass, being cancelled by Stanley Ho in

2008. Even though Stanley Ho did not end up with any floating or non-floating entertainment center, at least he was in some way announcing to the whole world that a promise given to him was not kept.

Most of the active names who took part in the first phase, the study for the plausibility of the casino setup of Project Varyag, had another common ground: Bill Clinton, then President of the United States!

The link between these people to Clinton was their illegal donations to Democratic Party and Clinton's election campaign via intermediaries. Because, according to American Federal Election Laws, foreigners were not allowed to donate to political parties or presidential candidates.

One of those intermediaries was Johnny Chung, who was found guilty of banking fraudulency, tax evasion, and violating election laws for his donation to the campaign. Chung was a short-term business partner of Liu Chaoying in California. Liu Chaoying had introduced Chung to Ji Shengde in Hong Kong. During this meeting, Ji said, "We love your president," to Chung, and assured him that he would get some money transferred to assist Clinton's re-election efforts. A few days after the meeting, Lieutenant Colonel Liu would switch 300,000 USD to a Hong Kong account of Chung. However, Chung spent most of it for his own businesses and donated only 35,000 USD to Clinton's election campaign.

The reason for Liu to support Clinton's re-election was satellite technology. This was one of the fields of expertise Liu Chaoying had in China Aerospace, and the Clinton administration had loosened export restrictions about China's satellite technology.

Another intermediary for the illegal donations was Yah-Lin "Charlie" Trie, an American citizen who ran a restaurant in Little Rock, Arkansas. Ng Lap Seng had transferred over one million USD from his Macau and Hong Kong accounts to Charlie Trie. Charlie Trie had funnelled it illegally to the Democratic National Committee, the Democratic Party's managing body during the Clinton administration. In late 1996, when the Congress hearings headed towards himself, Charlie Trie fled to China. After his return to the US in 1998, he was sentenced to four months of house arrest and three years of probation for violating federal campaign finance laws by donating to an election campaign on behalf of someone else and misinforming the Federal Election Commission.

His ten visits to the White House between 1994 and 1996 being well-known, Ng did not face any allegations regarding the illegal donations. Maintaining his life in Macau, he became a real estate billionaire, retaining his connections with top executives of the Chinese government and, possibly, intelligence services. Ng also preserved his interest in the United States, and between July 2013 and September 2015, he sent more than 4.5 million USD in cash to the US.

The intended purpose of this money came to light shortly. Being charged with bribing two United Nations ambassadors for their support for the conference center he was considering to build in Macau, Ng was arrested in September 2015, and one month later, released on a 50 million USD bail. His trial began in July 2017, and after five weeks of proceedings for six different crimes, including bribery, money laundering, and corruption, Ng was sentenced to serve four years.

With his wife and his partner, Chan Kai-kit attended Clinton's fundraising dinner at the Sheraton Hotel on May 13, 1996, among various donors.

Ng and Chan did not have any personal reasons to support Clinton. Everything was based on China's interests. In return for donating on several occasions heavily to the presidential candidates who appeared to follow policies in China's interests, they would obtain unofficial protection from the Chinese Army for their scandalous affairs in Macau. Nevertheless, this protection did not help Chan in August 1999. The Independent Commission Against Corruption of Hong Kong issued a statement seeking the arrest of eight people, including Chan, his wife Elsie Chan, his sibling, and his accountant. The allegation was that, in 1997 and 1998, Chan and his accomplices used letters of credit from various banks with fake documents of unreal transactions. This fraud had caused a 118.5 million Hong Kong dollars loss for Guangnan Holding. After all this, although his accomplices were caught and sentenced, Chan Kai-kit has never been captured and is still at large.

Stanley Ho was also among those who visited the White House in 1994. Ho had shaken hands with Bill Clinton and gave him a cheque worth 250 thousand USD for the Franklin Delano Roosevelt statue, which was planned to be built on Capitol Hill.

Ultimately, the Chinese government had a reason to support Clinton against his Republican opponent. Historically, China thought that a second term of the current president could be more lucrative for herself, rather than the possibility of facing a new president with an anti-China view.

Since the "Connections" behind the Project Varyag are explained in full detail, we can go back to the purchasing process and take a trip to Ukraine.

CHAPTER 3

PLAN B

Before discussing Varyag's purchase process in Ukraine, it is worth some time to become acquainted with Mykolaiv, the key center of Soviet-era shipbuilding, and in this context, with Ukraine itself.

Varyag was constructed in the city of Mykolaiv, also known as Nikolayev. Mykolaiv became one of the shipbuilding centers for the Soviets after the Great Patriotic War, when Soviet Union defended her lands against Nazi Germany and the other Axis countries. There are three large shipyards in Mykolaiv: Chernomorsky Shipbuilding Yard, 61 Communards Shipyards, and Okean Shipyard.

Founded in 1897, Chernomorsky Shipbuilding Yard, also known as the Black Sea Shipyard, is one of the largest shipyards in Europe. The yard has built a variety of vessel types in its history, including Admiral Kuznetsov, the only aircraft carrier Russian Navy has today, as well as various carriers, cruisers, destroyers, and submarines.

Mykolaiv remained a hidden city under a standard of high security for decades, until the breakup of the Soviet Union. The city was a forbidden zone, not only for tourists, but also for the relatives of the locals. In fact, any visitor would find themselves faced with military forces with machine guns. However, this rigour was not an insurmountable obstacle for US intelligence. Indeed, in 1984, KH-11 spy satellite pictures showing the construction of Kuznetsov at Chernomorsky Shipyard were leaked to the British military magazine Jane's

Defence Weekly. A civilian named Morison, hired by the US navy as an intelligence analyst, was convicted for espionage and embezzlement of government property and imprisoned for two years. Later, he was pardoned by President Bill Clinton in 2001.

The US maintained an interest in the shipyard during the breakup of the Soviet Union. It was stated on the November 28, 1991, issue of Inside the Pentagon, a weekly industry report on US Department of Defense policies, that the construction of two large aircraft carriers had been halted by Chernomorsky Shipyard. These carriers were the Riga (Varyag), which had been scheduled for commissioning in 1992, and the Ulyanovsk, which had been under construction since 1988. According to the insights of the military analysts in the said report, the halting would have no effect on US defense plans or security, for Soviet carriers were not then considered serious threats. Moreover, this proved the rapid decay of the Soviet defense industry, from previously having the power to produce weapons which posed a threat to US interests.

The process of disintegration accelerated under the policies of Glasnost and Perestroika (lucidity and restructuring) initiated by the Soviet Union after Mikhail Gorbachev was appointed the Secretary-General of the Communist Party in 1985, and nationalism flowered in Ukraine, as in all other former Soviet countries. Ukraine declared her segregation from the Soviet Union on August 24, 1991. After the foundation of Commonwealth of Independent States (CIS) by eleven former-Soviet countries and Gorbachev's resignation on December 25, 1991, the Soviet Union officially collapsed. Following these developments, Ukraine was seen as one of the countries with a higher chance of obtaining greater economic prosperity and integrating with Europe. However, towards the end of the twentieth century, the Ukrainian economy was faced with severe deterioration, with a level of social and political change that was insufficient to transform Ukraine into a European country.

PLAN B

The breakup of the Soviet Union had the ship industry officials in Mykolaiv re-focus on building for foreign markets. From then on, if Russia wanted aircraft carriers, she first had to be able to convince Ukraine, and then offer to buy those carriers. But instead of completed carriers, Russia was more interested in gaining control of the Black Sea fleet and Sevastopol, the Crimean coastal city where the fleet resided.

When Ukraine claimed the whole fleet, which had formed an important part of the Soviet naval force, Russia replied that "the fleet always belonged to Russia and always would be", raising tensions between two countries.

In June 1992, Ukrainian President Kravchuk and Russian President Boris Yeltsin reached an agreement, stating the fleet would have a joint administration for three years, to be shared accordingly afterwards. Further into the negotiations, Ukraine agreed to let Russia have majority shares of the fleet in return for acquitted debt. Following these developments, Russia made her final decision regarding Varyag in 1996. Due to limited government resources and Ukraine's estimated demand of high construction pricing, the carrier was entirely discarded. In 1997, another agreement was signed between the two states, permitting the Russian Black Sea Fleet to remain in Sevastopol until 2017. However, upon the referendum in Crimea to join Russia, and the outcome in favor, Russia annexed Crimea, which caused the process to take an utterly different turn.

The US did not consider carriers as a significant threat, but as of 1997, their interest for the shipyard persisted. It had been years since the satellite pictures of Kuznetsov, the carrier then being constructed, were published, but that incident recurred, and on January 1, 1997, a spy satellite picture of Varyag was published in the Washington Times. The picture was obtained from a "top secret" CIA report by journalist Bill Gertz. It showed the SA-N-9 surface-to-air missile system dismantled and left on Varyag's deck, as well as some of the equipment, including a special radar, on the dock. The report further stated that hatches on certain parts of the ship had been opened and the interior had been corroded. Apart from all these, the CIA mentioned in the report that Varyag had been sold to a European company and was expected to be moved to a ship-breaking facility in India.

This expectation of the CIA did not materialise. However, it was still not economically possible to complete the construction of the Varyag. Less than one year after the publication of that report, Ukrainian cabinet's National Agency for Reconstruction and Development (NARD) announced an international auction to sell the Varyag on December 1, 1997. NARD officials stated that defense industry experts estimated the ship's value at 20 million USD and expected around fifteen foreign companies to bid. Countries under UN embargo were not allowed to participate in the bidding. The bids would be admitted before February 1, 1998, and the result would be announced to the public by mid-March.

So, when exactly did Xu join in and how did he purchase the carrier? To answer these questions, one must first take a glance at Xu's series of interviews, previously mentioned in the chapter "Connections."

According to his statement, Xu Zengping had visited Ukraine in January 1998 to meet with government officials and shipbuilders. Conscious of the hardship, Xu got into very challenging negotiations. Taking the officials and builders to luxury dinners, he spared no expense for Varyag. In addition to rolls of money, he also served them erguotou, a very strong white liqueur from China with 62% alcohol by volume. Xu later admitted that with the Ukrainians, they would drink two to three litres of erguotou at every meal. However, he did not hesitate to add that his drinking was goal-directed; he believed the Ukrainians were drinking to get drunk, while he could keep a more sober mind.

At the end of the negotiations, Xu convinced Ukrainians to sell him the carrier and all her important blueprints for 20 million USD and made the necessary arrangements for money transfer. But what had seemed like a done deal wasn't, and in mid-February, Ukrainian officials announced that the carrier would be put up for open auction. Based on Xu's statement in the same interview, there were different countries interested in Varyag, and he had only three days to bid. And yet, far from hindering his plan, this alteration went in his favour.

With the help of Ukrainian businessmen with whom he formed close relations during his visit to the country, Xu prepared his documents in time and became the only bidder that met important requirements. As of March 19, 1998, Xu had outbid his opponents from the US, Australia, South Korea, and Japan and won the ship.

It is worth taking a break from the matter here and pointing out a few facts, because, as you have also noticed, when you consider the bidding process first by NARD's announcement and then Xu's interview, the dates seem to have some contradictions.

It is important to note that Xu's interview on SCMP was made seventeen years after his visit to Ukraine. This suggests two possibilities; Either he had a hard time remembering the dates, or he deliberately reflected it this way. If it is not simple confusion but deliberate action, then it may be claimed that the bidding process was fixed beforehand. That is to say, Xu might have visited Ukraine in the last quarter of 1997 (probably in October) and had had his negotiations before the bidding was announced. The high 20-million bidding price makes it likelier that Xu and the Ukrainian party had some pre-negotiation. This is because this price was three times the normal scrap price for carriers of this size, so it was quite unlikely for the price to go this high in a normal open bidding process without pre-negotiation.

In any case, the bidding was over. The National Agency for Reconstruction and European Integration (NAREI) sold the carrier on the condition that it would not be used for military purposes, acquitting themselves of any responsibilities.

Before long, however, the Far Eastern Economic Review (FEER) of Hong Kong, then one of the prominent press outlets in Asia, wrote that Chong Lot was a subsidiary of the Hong-Kong operated company Chinluck and had connections with the PLA. Whereupon the Kyiv Post, Ukranian's oldest English-language newspaper, started asking some questions to NAREI. Spokesperson Roksolana Protskiv answered these questions via fax, claiming that the bidding committee was not aware of Chong Lot's connection with the Chinese army, and the agency had only fulfilled its mission, having no authority to take further actions. The spokesperson did not answer the question as to why an agency interested in economic recovery and European integration, unrelated to defense or shipping, had been chosen to sell the Varyag. Chinese diplomats in Kiev, on the other hand, emphasized that Beijing had nothing to do with the purchase of Varyag and that the buyers were of Macau origin. The Embassy's media advisor Chen Tsingsyn stated that they were not responsible for Macau citizens' commercial activities, adding that Macau would only be a part of PRC from December 20, 1999, onwards.

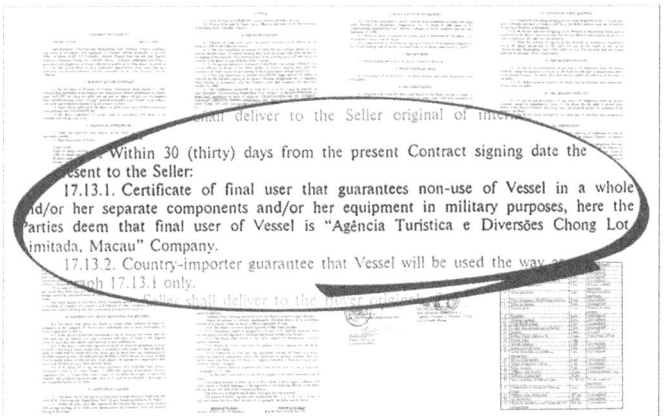

Contract of purchase and sale between Chernomorsky Shipbuilding Yard as the "Seller" and Agência Turística e Diversões Chong Lot Limitada as the "Buyer".

PLAN B

Xu's statements about the purchasing process so far are partly convincing, though the rest is far from that.

To look back at his statements regarding this process, according to his words, a helicopter of unknown origin landed on Varyag's deck on the night of the bidding. Xu says that he does not know to whom the helicopter belonged, but that he was suspicious of certain sources. As a matter of fact, the very next day, forty tons of layout prints from the carrier were loaded hastily, in a sort of panic, onto eight trucks to be sent to China.

Now the main part of the business had been done, leaving only the payment to be made. According to Xu, he was not able to complete the payment for a year because of the Asian Financial Crisis. He made the last payment with a default interest of 10 million USD on April 30, 1999, and became the sole owner of the carrier.

But why are these facts not reliable enough? To see the answer, one ought to track down the money.

It was previously stated that in 1997, Xu had collateralised his land to take a loan from CASIL Clearing, owned entirely by Lieutenant Colonel Liu Chaoying's CASIL. But Xu apparently was not considering taking his land back, as he had not paid his debt. In fact, in 2004, Xu filed a lawsuit against CASIL Clearing, claiming that the company failed to provide a total of 330 million Hong Kong dollars needed to pay Chinluck, in accordance with the contract. CASIL Clearing objected to the claim, countersuing for the repayment of the 251.5 million Hong Kong dollars loan with interest.

In December 2006, the court ruled that CASIL Clearing would pay Chinluck a nominal penalty of 100 (one hundred) Hong Kong dollars for the breach of contract, and that Chinluck would also pay both the capital and the accrued interest which remained unpaid despite the loan agreement and mortgage.

In September 2007, CASIL Clearing reached an agreement with Xu to settle altogether. According to the agreement, Xu agreed to pay 280 million Hong Kong dollars by instalments back to CASIL Clearing. Paying the last instalment in the first half of 2011, he cleared his debt to CASIL Clearing and got his land back on the island of Peng Chau.

By rough estimate, Xu must have needed a total of 30 to 35 million USD, for activities including the company formation in Macau, the offices that were opened in Kiev and Beijing to deal with ship purchasing, the expenses to convince Ukrainians, the purchase of the carrier and its towage by tugboats from Ukraine to China, and the passing tolls of Turkish Straits. His initial source, the amount he had taken from CASIL Clearing was approximately 32.5 million USD by the exchange rate of the year and was barely enough for the cost of Project Varyag.

However, Xu must have foreseen that the said amount of money would not be enough to purchase the carrier, so he went on to look for new financial sources. As previously mentioned, his second source was a colleague from Hong Kong.

The person, whom Xu mentioned as his "friend", was Shao Chun, the chairman of state-controlled China Securities Co. Ltd. (CSC) or, by its Chinese name, Huaxia Securities, from Beijing. CSC also has a subsidiary called China Securities (International) Ltd. (CSCI) that was based in Hong Kong since 1994. Actually, Shao Chun was not Hong Kongese, contrary to Xu's claim, but Chinese, born in 1944 in Beijing. Since we took it in stride when Xu confused the dates, we could also overlook his confusion regarding his friend's origin, could we not?

The important thing here is the inception of Xu and Shao's acquaintance. Xu was introduced to Shao by executives of the company Beijing Taixinda Technology Development Limited, to which he applied for financial support. Taixinda Technology was a small size tech company founded by Wu Wei in August 1997 in Beijing. Interestingly, within their first year, the two new partners had joined Taixinda Technology's managerial board – without investing capital. Had it been Wu Wei's own call to get partners for his company, or had some party picked them for him? The answer is not clear. But Wu Wei was somehow introduced by his partners, first with Shao Chun, and then Xu Zengping. Xu was looking for funds for his project and Shao's company had it. Wishing to expand his company, Wu Wei suddenly found himself accepted within Project Varyag. Taixinda Technology would act as the intermediary company between Chinluck and CSC.

Therefore, Xu had told Shao about Project Varyag, stating his need for "national and special operations," in order to obtain a loan of 80 million yuan from CSC via Taixinda Technology, while promising financial gains for CSC.

With Shao's loan to Xu, more new names enrolled in the project. Among them were Li Bin, a partner of Wu Wei, and Wu Yu, CSC's fund management department deputy manager. Another name was Zhang Yong. Born in 1938, in Penglai city of Shandong province, Zhang Yong moved to Hong Kong in 1989 to get a permanent residence permit. Here he was the chairman and general manager of Goldspot Investment Limited (Chinese name: Dacheng Investment Co. Ltd.) which he himself formed in 1993. Zhang's Goldspot had few employees and was operating in a small office at Bonham Trade Center.

From here on, you will also read some quotations from an article of China International News Media, dated November 29, 2018, which was citing the interview of PLAN's political writer, Li Zhongxiao, with Zhang Yong, an individual who made an undeniable contribution to the Project Varyag.

According to the article, Shao Chun met Zhang Yong via Wu Wei in August 1998 in Beijing. Shao wanted Zhang to enrich CSC with a different point of views and offered to cover all his expenses. Upon his acceptance, Zhang was appointed as CSC's Hong Kong correspondent from October 1998. In later meetings, Shao would tell Chang that the main issue was Project Varyag and reiterate the importance of its secrecy.

According to the same article, when Shao had just decided to move forward with Zhang, Xu once again visited Shao and asked for another 150 million yuan to move Varyag at the end of October 1998. When Shao wanted him to show the official documents also known as "red-headed docs", Xu told him they were state secrets, that he could not share them, but that he could introduce him to the relevant person.

Indeed, Shao Chun had met with Vice Admiral He Pengfei via Xu. However, what Shao learned from He, had nothing to do with Xu. He Pengfei told him that there was no such document since this was not a government business. He also added that this non-government plan was a special operation, a one-time only opportunity and that he hoped Xu would purchase Varyag.

Shao was impressed by He's words and decided to maintain his support for Xu's carrier purchase. As a result, CSC had transferred another 150 million yuan via Taixinda Technology on October 29, 1998. An amount of five million from this money was subtracted by Wu Wei as an intermediation service fee, and the rest was sent to Chinluck's Shenzhen Office account by four separate interactions.

At the end of October 1998, Varyag had not weighed anchor from Chernomorsky Shipyard in Ukraine. Upon hearing no word from Xu, Shao sent Zhang over to him to find out what was happening. Xu claimed that expenses were too much and asked for 900 thousand USD more. This request had put Zhang into a dilemma. If he would not send the money, Varyag would not get under way. On the other hand, if he did, there was also no guarantee that she would ever get under way either. Consequently, Zhang told Xu, "You cannot maintain the project," before adding, "Beijing" – meaning Shao – "has lost its confidence in you."

Having rejected the demands of Shao early on to have his accounts checked, Xu had to reveal many documents of his bank accounts when Zhang forced him. Xu must have thought that these documents, mostly written in a foreign language, would be unintelligible. But things did not go as he hoped, and it was detected that the last payment of 145 million Chinese yuan, that he had received from CSC via Taixinda Technology, was not registered in company accounting entries.

As seen from Zhang's statements, Xu had abused the confidence shown to him. CSC, along with the 80 million paid before, had supported the project with 230 million yuan (approx. 27.77 million USD) only to fill Xu's pockets.

In rough estimate, Xu had nearly 60 million USD in his pocket for certain. It is also possible that about 12 million of the related amounts could have been paid to the Chernomorsky Shipyard, based on a letter of reprimand sent by the shipyard. It is reasonable to assume that some slight amount was spent for simple expenses, such as company formation etc. But did Xu use the rest to purchase the ship? Answering this question with a "yes" is hardly possible.

So, what did Xu really do with the money? His most interesting purchase was a villa in Hong Kong. Xu had purchased the luxury estate known as the Versailles Palace of Hong Kong in an auction held by National Electronic Holding for 250 million Hong Kong dollars (approx. 32.27 million USD).

Xu considered the villa a display of status to Hong Kong's elite. Having a Victorian design which made the villa look a hundred years old, it was a three-storey building with seven bedrooms, built on four acres of land. The fifteen-feet-high living room was the most extravagant part of the house. The floor was tiled with French oak to go with a classical outlook; there was also a swimming pool with snail-shaped fountains. The facade had elegant Roman columns.

A fan of showing off, Xu had rented the villa in the last quarter of 1999 for an award ceremony of Metro Radio, and after a thorough renovation, he sold it less than one year later to Chinese businessman Cheng Lu for 260 million Hong Kong dollars.

According to his own words, Xu had made the last payment for the ship on April 30, 1999. Hence, his claim that he completed the money required for Varyag with his villa – "I sold it as the third financial source," he said – falls wide of the mark. On the contrary, Xu had bought the villa with the largest part of what he borrowed for the carrier's purchase.

As motivations, a fondness for luxury or a quest for stature would prove too simple to explain Xu's loose handling of a duty made in partnership with such an uncompromising institute as the Chinese army. Beneath this conduct was a situation, unknown to anyone within the project. A setback had occurred that led this entrepreneur to believe that Project Varyag could never be completed. As will be explained further, obtaining permission to pass Varyag through Turkish Straits had turned into quite a thorny process. Immediately after winning the bidding, Xu made a contract with Fairmount Marine in 1998, a Rotterdam-based towage company, to tow Varyag from Mykolaiv to Macau, and also made a request for transit to Turkey via an agency of this company; however, this request was rejected. Xu understood from this refusal that the project would ultimately fail, and, according to this article, had then decided to keep what he could for himself. He had a substantial amount already collected for Varyag. If he had notified the planners of the project about this refusal, he would have been obliged to refund it. Why should he have done this when he could instead use this amount to make a gain? He could have thought that he would return the money to its spenders after he himself made some profit and acquired some status for himself in Hong Kong. This seems like the probable root cause behind Xu's dereliction of his duty.

To turn back to the article; having decided that he was being deceived, Shao suggested that Goldspot should become a subsidiary of China Securities (International) Ltd, and Xu's Chong Lot shares should be transferred to this company. Upon Zhang's approval, formalities were followed through in March 1999, and Goldspot became a subsidiary of CSCI. In the upcoming days, Zhang would go on to rapidly reduce his company's other workload. Also, the same month, Shao had begun to look for partners to supply the necessary funds to complete the project and to this end, made an offer to Dongfang Huizhong Investment Holding Co. Ltd. (Chinese name: Oriental Exchange Investment Holdings Limited).

This was Plan B. Although it was normal for Shao to be on the market since he lost CSC's money, it does not seem logical to think that he made and executed such a plan on his own. Therefore, Shao did not have much of an option but to reach out to Vice Admiral He Pengfei. If he used the legal route to file a complaint about Xu, he could find himself in some tangle in which he could be labelled as a traitor. Things were not much different for He Pengfei, either. It became a necessity to take Xu out and invite new names into Project Varyag.

The company Shao invited was Dongfang Huizhong, which supports the theory that He Pengfei was the name behind Plan B. This is because Dongfang Huizhang was no ordinary organization. It was a subsidiary of the Chinese National Defense and Transportation Union, chaired by Major General Gao Zengxia. There was also a strong possibility that Gao could have taken part in the preliminary works for China's Varyag quest, along with Vice Admiral He Pengfei and Major General Ji Shengde.

Dongfang Huizhong called Shao back immediately and informed him that they wanted to take part in Project Varyag. Soon afterwards, a letter of reprimand sent by Chernomorsky Shipyard arrived at Chong Lot in April 1999. Accordingly, Ukraine was urging Chong Lot to pay 13 million USD: 8 million of which is the unpaid amount of Varyag's 20 million USD bidding price, and 5 million for default interest and fines. Unless the debt was paid before April 30, the contract would be terminated, and previous payments could not be refunded.

Ukraine's reprimand accelerated the process and after two weeks of tough negotiations regarding share transferring, Xu agreed to transfer 80% of Chong Lot to Goldspot.

Even though Xu, at first glance, seemed to be backed into a corner and desperately accepted the share transfer, things were not quite so. Examining a letterhead document dated April 19,

1999, adorned with the signature of Xu Zengping from Chinluck Holding Company Limited, reveals Xu's adeptness at capitalizing on opportunities to generate profit.

Having determined the value of Chong Lot as 60 million USD, Xu was asking for 48 million for his 80% share. Moreover, he had not forgotten his 230-million-yuan loan from CSC, deducting the 25.56 million USD equivalent from the total. However, calculating an exchange rate of 9 instead of 8.28, he looked out for himself once again. Xu also wanted the 13 million USD for the shipyard at Goldspot's own expense, and he had given up on that amount as well. After deducting these figures, he demanded the 9.44 million USD to be transferred to his account in three months. Therefore, creditor CSC had suddenly become the debtor.

On April 29, 1999, majority shares of Chong Lot tourist and Amusement Agency Limited were transferred to Goldspot Investment Limited in Macau, in the presence of Notary Paula Ling. New share distribution of Chong Lot was as follows: 80% Goldspot Investment Limited, 18% Xu Zengping, and 2% Chong, Lap Cheung. Also with this shift, Goldspot officials Zhang Yong, Wu Wei and Wu Yu became board members. Despite retaining only, a minority share, Xu retained his post as the general manager, with Wu Wei as the newly appointed vice general manager.

As mentioned in the article, Goldspot – and subsequently, CSC – had gained 80% of the shares, but it also would assume responsibility for the 13 million USD debt. Thus, on April 30, the deadline date of the payment, Zhang Yong was obliged to send 8 million USD to Ukraine. The disturbance caused by these incident and similar events would end Xu's time as general manager. Indeed, in two meetings in August and October 1999, Xu first lost his title, then his directorship duties as a whole. In other words, Xu would not be able to carry out Chong Lot's businesses.

Whether international intelligence services detected this share transfer immediately or not remains unknown, but it took

PLAN B

a while for it to be reflected in the media. The newspaper SCMP, with its story "Beijing Calms Waters for Floating Casino" published on September 9, 2001, by Adam Luck and Raymond Ma, announced that Goldspot had bought Chong Lot's majority shares in 1999. Tracing Goldspot's steps, the journalists had also managed to reveal that although Guo Dan and Luo Xianping appeared to be the directors, the majority shareholder was CSC's Hong Kong subsidiary China Securities (International) Limited.

At this point, this question aptly comes to mind: "Why is Zhang Yong's name not among the Goldspot managers?" To answer this, it is worth taking a look at Goldspot's records on Companies Registry (CR), a government department under the Financial Services and the Treasury Bureau of the Government of Hong Kong for business registration and business management purposes.

According to a "notification of secretarial and administrative changes" dated March 28, 1999, all the directors except Zhang Yong resigned; Wu Wei, Wu Yu and Li Bin were appointed as new directors. Also, an address declaration form dated March 31 shows that the company address was changed to Gloucester Tower. After these developments, a later notification of change dated November 27, 1999, showed that, along with Wu Wei and Li Bin, Zhang Yong also resigned as director; and in their stead, Guo Dan and Luo Xianping were appointed. Yet Wu Yu's resignation took place on April 17, 2001.

When journalists published their story in September 2001, the administrative changes had long since happened, and by this means the roles of Zhang Yong, Wu Wei and Wu Yu in the project remained secret. Now they were only Chong Lot's board members and were not deemed important anymore. However, there was another significant point the journalists had uncovered: Lou Xianping's Beijing address was shown to be in the residential area of the People's Armed Police, a paramilitary force of the PLA.

It would not be an exaggeration to claim that this story was quite effective in increasing worries in the international arena about whether Varyag was not purchased as a floating casino, but to be used as an aircraft carrier. Journalists had a massive success with this story which they published unaware that majority share transfer to Goldspot meant that "Plan B" was in motion. The executors of Plan B had not foreseen this either. For if the Xu-centered plan had not failed, such a situation would not have arisen, and the notion of a carrier-turned-into-floating-casino would retain its weight. But now that the genie was out, the world was talking about the possibility of Varyag becoming China's first carrier.

To turn back to the course of events, we should first discuss Dongfang Huizhong's role in this story. It is possible to find out why this peripherally mentioned company became involved, by looking at the China International New Media article penned by Xiang Ruicheng on January 17, 2017.

According to the article, during the mutual negotiations over Dongfang Huizhong's wish to join in Project Varyag, by not refusing Shao's offer, it was decided that Goldspot would take over 80% shares of Chong Lot to give Dongfang Huizhong, and in return Dongfang Huizhong would take over Chong Lot's whole debt; and a contract was signed accordingly.

As it is easily understood, the 80% share transfer Xu agreed took place upon Dongfang Huizhong's request and, therefore, was a part of He Pengfei's Plan B.

During the negotiations between Shao and Dongfang Huizhong there was one more name other than the chairman Gao Zengxia and top-level officials, and who was appointed as Dongfang Huizhong's Project Varyag delegate: General Manager Dai Yue.

At the time of mutual agreement, the Second Department of the PLA General Staff Headquarters, which was in charge of intelligence, suddenly became involved in the business. They were involved by Liu Xingyuan, who was the chairman of

Xinghaoyuan Investment & Development. He had business relations with Dongfang Huizhong and then connected with the General Staff's Second Department. He reported this situation to the Second Department's leaders.

With that, the Beijing Bureau administration, along with Major General Gu Gaoqiang in administration, stated that they would support Dongfang Huizhong in Project Varyag. With the Second Department's involvement, Liu Xingyuan replaced Gao Zengxia in June 1999 to become not only the chairman of Dongfang Huizhong, but also the Army's intermediary. Liu was both the leader of the project and was also directly reporting to the General Staff's Second Department. General Manager Dai Yue was appointed as the Second Department's "trustworthy business partner", while Zhang Yong became the vice general manager.

Dongfang Huizhong's new administration was swift to take certain decisions to manage the process. Initially, the plan to transform the carrier by the shell company Chong Lot would stay in course. But then, to obtain technical drawings and to gather materials, Ukrainian professional and technical staff would be lured in, and a fund would be launched for the project to find investors for Wugui Highway and Southwest Pharmaceutical Company projects. The delegation who would visit Ukraine to purchase the carrier would include Dai Yue and Zhang Yong, as well as a lawyer, a technical advisor, and an interpreter.

The delegation encountered several obstacles in the form of late payments on their first Ukraine visit in late August. After the completion of purchase transactions, a handover ceremony was arranged on October 24, 1999.

Varyag's handover document was signed between Chernomorsky Shipyard Chairman of the Board Thionenko, and Chong Lot delegates Dai Yue and Zhang Yong. Dated October 24, 1999, a document numbered "775/01", listed certain articles with conditions apropos of the carrier's preparation for civilian usage and preservation – as long as the carrier remained in the shipyard, five thousand USD would be paid per day. But regardless of terms, Varyag had finally fallen into Chinese hands!

When the delegation returned from Ukraine in November, Shao had changed his attitude toward the project, and despite the contract, had not transferred the shares. Furthermore, he had requested Dongfang Huizhong's rights to conduct the project and Varyag's ownership in regard to CSC. However, Liu, the chairman of Dongfang Guizhong, having not received any commands from his superiors, acted according to the original business model.

But why had Shao changed his attitude? The reason is that, as previously mentioned, when Dongfang Huizhong looked for investors to create funds for the project, the Hong Kong-based "New China Company" was one of the applicants. This company had brought a letter of guarantee that was valued at 800 million Taiwan dollars (approx. 26.06 million USD) from a Taiwan bank to prove their financial reliability to Dongfang Huizhong. This previously unknown company's high-valued guarantee letter prompted Dongfang Huizhong to act cautiously, and Zhang Yong was appointed to conduct a private investigation in Hong Kong, whereupon the company turned out to be on paper only, its financial position even more inconsistent than it looked, and the talks broke off altogether.

Hearing about this development, yet entirely misunderstanding and asking nothing to Dongfang Huizhong, Shao filed a report directly to the Army, stating that Dongfang Huizhong sold the carrier to Taiwan.

In this way, the top-secret Project Varyag was uncovered and caught the attention of top-level authorities. It was now inevitable for a crisis to occur within government ranks.

This exposure led to a joint investigation by the Central Commission for Discipline Inspection, Beijing Financial Business Commission, Ministry of Public Security's Financial Investigation Office, and Beijing Financial Investigation Office. By April 2000, Chairman Liu Xingyuan, General

Manager Dai Yue, and the lawyer of the delegation that visited Ukraine were all arrested.

Eventually the investigation showed the report's content was unfounded, but the investigating board also ran a general investigation on Dongfang Huizhong about Project Varyag. Over the course of events, Major General Gu Gaoqiang, the administrator of the Beijing Office, found that he had a spot of bother with his superiors regarding the project, and this led to his resignation. His replacement, Wang Xianpeng, denied both Liu Xingyuan's involvement with the project, and the fact that Dongfang Huizhong was involved in the project with government approval. Wang Xianpeng claimed the project was a rogue "private operation" and opened an investigation into the company.

Within this detailed investigation, a report of the project was submitted to PLAN commanders, including Admiral Shi Yunsheng and Deputy Commander He Pengfei; the latter admitted to their awareness of the project, but added that the Naval Party Committee did not sponsor the project. Eventually, the investigation board presented the comprehensive report to the central government's attention. The central government published an extensive notice regarding the subject, underlying that "this is not an exemplary situation, such circumstances should not occur ever again, and only the government should be responsible for such projects."

In accordance with this notice, the investigation board concluded Dongfang Huizhong was operating illegally, without performing his legal obligations, yet still found the conspiracy claims too weak. That is why the mentioned names had their investigations and custodies removed. The company acted immediately when they were asked to hand the project over to government authorities. The handover was completed when Zhang Yong got all the documents of Project Varyag and submitted them, along with Chong Lot's seal, to the Second Department of the General Staff Department.

VARYAG

The Second Department handed all the documents including the purchase contract and the company seal over, in a formal ceremony, to China Shipbuilding Industry, Inc. on April 8, 2000.

Zhang Yong, who had not taken part in that ceremony, had one last mission to undertake for the project: To sign a certificate of authority for Mou Ancheng, the chief engineer of China Shipbuilding Industry, Inc., and also the Director of Military Industry Office, and his deputy Hu Jizheng. Going to Macau without any delay, Zhang signed the paper in a law office, and with that action, brought Project Varyag's first phase to a close.

Those readers who are familiar with Chinese bureaucracy will see that it appears that the crisis was avoided a little too easily. Could this action, taken in spite of Jiang Zemin, the head of Chinese Communist Party (CCP), China People's Liberation Army and People's Republic of China, remain unpunished, and on top of it, could it be possible for this project to just be handed over to the government?

To answer this correctly, some clarification needs to be made regarding the reason behind Jiang Zemin's opposition to Varyag's addition to the Chinese Navy.

Considering all the points, it could very well be said that there was a lobby within the Chinese Navy led by Admiral Liu Huaqing which acted to bring China an aircraft carrier. And it is very clear that this request of the PLAN lobby would mean that China could become a deterrent superpower in Taiwan and South China Sea.

Nevertheless, during his presidencies, Jiang Zemin adopted a "peaceful growth" view to dissipate the fear of China's rising power. On his terms, China established tight diplomacy with neighbours, attempting to mend relations with Asian neighbours and, after Tiananmen, to improve the country's image. This is why Jiang Zemin objected to the purchase of the aircraft carrier. The President worked hard to build an image of China. He did not want that image to suffer any harm.

PLAN B

Jiang Zemin was not the sole person who decided against a carrier. When Deng Xiaoping, who had taken up the reins after Mao, handed the power over to Jiang Zemin, the era of charismatic leaders had ended, and despite the hierarchy, all decisions began to be made by the seven members of CCP Politburo Standing Committee. So, this was also that think-tank's refusal.

Interestingly, when this decision was taken between 1992 and 1997, Liu Huaqing was also among those committee members. Even if we could not know of Liu Huaqing's attitude in the committee, when the carrier lobby had their demands rejected, they decided to run and maintain Project Varyag in secret. Right until Shao misunderstood (?) everything and complained to the Army that the carrier was sold to Taiwan.

Coincidence that, Jiang Zemin was also known for his hawkish attitude towards Taiwan, the island he defined as China's secessionist part. Apparently, Shao's complaint was part of Plan B, plotted to convince the Politburo Standing Committee (1997-2002) which involved Jiang Zemin, about Project Varyag. When Taiwan was mentioned, the matter became indisputable, and no one was punished.

Even though Liu Huaqing, who died in 2011, had previously been the last military-origin member of the Politburo Standing Committee, he only managed to get his wish from the committee when he was no longer a member. Thus, the Chinese People's Liberation Army Navy's dream of an aircraft carrier, as a part of their longing for a blue water navy was on the verge of coming true. And the carrier was indeed purchased with Zhang's laudable efforts, in spite of Xu's assorted misconducts.

But the aftereffects were not quite smooth, either. Varyag still had a long journey ahead. This giant aircraft carrier would have to pass through Turkish Straits, experiencing many more gruelling adventures. But this time she would have the power of the state of China behind her, and she was ready to sail into wilder waters!

CHAPTER 4

SLOW BOAT

Have you ever heard the idiom, "on a slow boat to China"? This Western idiom means "taking a long time", "as if coming from the far end of the world" or "for an interminable time." Varyag's voyage, which was expected to be a leisurely 60-day trip instead lasted 627, was an embodiment of this idiom. Any look at this seemingly never-ending voyage from Mykolaiv would prove this ascription right. As you may recall, on April 29, 1999, the majority shares of Chong Lot were transferred to Goldspot, and the next day, Xu Zengping's principal debt to Chernomorsky Shipyard was paid off. And the first steps of Plan B were taken in March, with the decision to exclude Xu.

One of the next things to do was determining the contractor company for Varyag's towing. International Transport Contractors, a big Dutch towage and salvage company, was tailor made for this. ITC had a solid reputation, with long experience in ocean towage on a world-wide basis. Upon negotiations with the CEO Joop Timmermans and ITC's commercial and operational staff, a contract was signed between Chong Lot and ITC in April 1999 for Varyag's towing to Macau. To begin the voyage, ITC's tug Sable Cape reached Mykolaiv on April 25.

However, nothing would go as planned. It came to light that the official contract regarding Varyag's purchase had not been signed, and furthermore, various formalities including shipbuilding document, ownership certificate were incomplete.

VARYAG

Apparently, not only were payments needed, but also, Xu had made no effort to obtain necessary documents for the carrier to be towed through international waters by a tug. Legal issues piled on top of the financial issues with the shipyard, which meant Sable Cape could not tow Varyag.

The tug waited in the shipyard for six months, until the delegation with Dai Yue and Zhang Yong arrived at Ukraine in October 1999, only to then send away the tugboat due to further delays in the process. Sable Cape departed from Mykolaiv on 9 November 1999 with destination Singapore.

When the shipyard's requests were met, and Varyag was handed over to China Shipbuilding Industry, Inc., ITC was once again invited to Mykolaiv. On June 14, 2000, early in the morning, Varyag left Chernomorsky Shipyard under the control of ITC's tug Suhaili, never to return. The fraught voyage to Macau, through the Turkish Straits and the Suez Canal, had begun.

The Dnieper-Bug estuary canal, connecting the shipyard to the Black Sea, was the first stage of the voyage. Temporarily closed to traffic before every midnight, this canal received a base scan beforehand, and buoys were placed throughout the passageway. During the passage, Suhaili was accompanied by two other tugs: Tigris and Balast. Because of the sudden winds often faced on these waters, the almost quarter-mile convoy navigated at four miles per hour and completed the passage in twelve long hours. They sailed smoothly until the Black Sea entrance, after which the two assisting tugs left the convoy.

The Turkish Straits, consisting of the Bosphorus, the Sea of Marmara, and the Dardanelles (Canakkale Strait), was the next destination of Suhaili with Varyag on her tow line, but first the Black Sea had to be traversed. Located on the south-eastern fringe of Europe, the Black Sea is a 131,200 cubic-mile inland sea, surrounded by Ukraine, Russia, Georgia, Turkey, Bulgaria, and Romania, connected with the Mediterranean Sea through the Turkish Straits. Therefore, the Turkish Straits were the only departure route for Varyag to reach her new home.

However, only twenty-eight hours had passed since the carrier had set sail, when an accident occurred, and it constituted the first ring on the chain of misfortunes that would continue throughout the voyage. Suhaili, after having a failure in the starboard engine, had to carry on towing Varyag with her port side engine. ITC sent their own tug Sandy Cape off from Rotterdam for the towing to continue without halting, also renting the Ukraine-based tug Champion to be sent to the Suhaili and Varyag.

Varyag under tow by the tug Suhaili. *Photo from the album of Joop Timmermans.*

Suhaili and Varyag arrived at the Bosphorus three days after leaving Ukraine. In the meantime, China had instructed ITC to remain in the Black Sea. So, they waited in the Black Sea, for no apparent reason, until the early morning of June 20, when the tug Champion joined the other two. According to the contract between Chong Lot and ITC, Chong Lot must have gotten the passing clearance through the straits before Varyag left Mykolaiv. But China had misguided ITC and sought to make the pass a fait accompli by bringing Varyag near Bosphorus. Of course, things did not go that smoothly. The first application via an agency to the Turkish Undersecretariat of Maritime Affairs' Istanbul District Office was rejected. Thus, the second ring of the chain, Varyag's gloomy wait in Black Sea began. Since this giant carrier could not return to Mykolaiv either, she would spend more than sixteen months circling around Black Sea. After being towed from a Ukrainian dock, Varyag became the whole world's center of attention in this inland sea, which had long ago been named "black" from the winter storms that made its waters look dark. Diplomatic relations between Turkey and China would reach a new dimension in these sixteen months. At this point, we should explain what was behind this long process in which Varyag's Bosphorus passage was not allowed.

The objection to the passage of Varyag was not a direct call that could be made by the Istanbul District Office. Varyag's inability to move on her own was deemed a danger for the straits, and the Varyag having been built as an aircraft carrier raised further questions. A survey of past district office decisions showed that an application for a carrier to pass through Turkish Straits was not the first of its kind. However, as outlined in the previous chapter, everything about Xu's project had been kept under wraps, and his representations and misrepresentations had to be considered when assessing the situation. In these confused circumstances, the opinion of Maritime Affairs had to be sought. Accordingly, a meeting of experts took place, presided by Istanbul District Manager Ruhan Cakiroglu, who, along with his expertise of the industry, was well-known for his consistent and sturdy stance. The outcome was that a safe passage through the Turkish Straits for this floating mass which could only be moved by towing would not be possible.

The Bosphorus, connects the Black Sea with the Sea of Marmara. It separates Asia and Europe, bending itself around the most beautiful historical places of Istanbul, a city with a 3,000-year history, and, as of the year 2000, with a population of 11 million people. The Bosphorus Strait has a length of

19.56 miles, it is 2.92 miles wide at the Black Sea entrance and is approximately 1.55 miles wide at the Marmara entrance, and its narrowest point is 2,293 feet wide. The Varyag was 1,004 feet long and its convoy would stretch to almost 1,640 feet, with escorting tugs. That would require twelve sharp turns on the Bosphorus, four of them being ninety-degrees. A possible collision or running ashore due to the convoy length could cause the Bosphorus, which was constantly under high risk of accidents, to be closed for traffic indefinitely. Such an accident would not only have a negative impact on all the countries – especially those bordering on the Black Sea – that benefited from the Bosphorus, but also the strait itself could face the danger of losing its status as a corridor for marine biological life.

Istanbul and the Bosphorus, Turkey: The Crossroads of Europe and Asia. *Image by NASA.*

VARYAG

During the District Office meeting, Varyag was not considered a carrier, since a giant floating mass which was not completely built, and lacked both a motor, and steering gear, could not be classified as such. China, until this point presenting the purchase as non-military, now found itself in another kind of definitional stalemate. If Varyag was considered a carrier, then it would be questioned whether she was a commercial ship or a warship, thus her future would become a mare's nest. That is to say, although she was sold by Ukraine on the condition that she would not be used for military purposes, since she was built for exactly such a purpose and having no modifications for civilian utilisation, Varyag would have to be returned to Ukraine, or China would have to abandon her, in the event of her evaluation as a warship instead of a commercial ship. Because, according to the Montreux Convention Regarding the Regime of the Straits, signed by Turkey, Soviet Union, Bulgaria, Romania, England, France, Japan, Yugoslavia, and Greece in 1936, warships belonging to countries without a coast on the Black Sea could not remain in this sea for more than 21 days, and warships over 15 thousand tons belonging to countries with or without a Black Sea coast could not pass Turkish Straits – with one exception. Before elaborating this exception, it would be worth taking a look at the aforementioned convention.

The Montreux Convention is one of the rare multilateral conventions still in force since its signature date. While Italy signed it in 1938, Japan waived all its rights and benefits from it in 1951. Russia and Ukraine, as successors of the Soviet Union, gained "state party" status, whereas Georgia did not make any such demand. Recognising Turkey's sovereignty upon Turkish Straits, this convention mainly aimed to ensure the safety of Turkey and all the other states with Black Sea coasts. With this, commercial ships were granted a liberty to pass the straits, warships' passage during wartime and peacetime was regulated in accordance with states having coasts in Black Sea or not, also various restrictions regarding tonnage, timing and passage limitations were set forth. The execution and supervision of this regime has been granted to Turkey.

There are certain regulations in the Montreux Convention about environmental security and cruise safety on Turkish Straits. However, cruise safety constitutes an indispensable element of the passage liberty provided in the convention. Thus, Turkey has the jurisdiction to regulate passage safety in accordance with international law provisions or generally accepted agreements and contracts, and in this context, "Maritime Traffic Regulations for the Turkish Straits" were put in effect in 1994 and readjusted in 1998.

There is a relevant exception here... the Montreux Convention exceptionally allows the states that have coasts in the Black Sea to pass their "capital ships" over 10 thousand tons of displacement through the Turkish Straits. Capital ships are among navies' most important warships and the primary of a fleet. The convention does not explicitly define aircraft carriers as capital ships and contains no restriction specifically regarding them. But modern aircraft carriers, by their nature, weigh much more than the 15 thousand tons limit applied to warships, therefore it is impossible for them to pass through the straits.

What about the aircraft carriers which served the Soviet navy during the Soviet Union era, and afterwards the Russian navy? Were they ever able to pass through Turkish Straits? Aircraft carriers of the Soviet navy indeed were. The first was in 1976, Kiev, the Kiev class carrier, and then in 1991, Admiral Kuznetsov, the Kuznetsov class carrier passed from the Black Sea to the Mediterranean. Used against land and sea targets, and armed with various ballistic missiles, cannons and torpedo systems, Kiev and Kuznetsov class carriers were classified as "heavy aircraft cruisers" while getting built. This classification allowed them to be accepted as capital ships, and to pass through Turkish Straits in accordance with Montreux Convention provisions. Indeed, the convention states that, "the fitting of a landing-on or flying-off deck on any vessel of war, provided such vessel has not been designed or adapted primarily for the purpose of carrying and operating aircraft at sea, shall not cause any vessel to fit to be classified in the category of aircraft carrier."

The decision to disallow the passage of Varyag was taken according to the Montreux Convention and the International Maritime Organisation (IMO), in which Turkey is a state party. When the decision was disclosed to the applying agency, it was also stated that Varyag ought to be towed out of Turkish territorial waters. With that, Varyag was towed out by Suhaili and Champion back into the Black Sea. Upon Sandy Cape's arrival to Black Sea on June 29, Champion had fulfilled her duty and was duly released. On the other hand, Suhaili was relieved from Sandy Cape and Varyag on July 18 to be inspected by insurance experts and an ITC inspector, all of them having just arrived at Istanbul. According to additional requirements of the insurance policy, ITC this time dispatched Sumatras, a tug then residing on the Indian Ocean. After Sumatras reached Black Sea on July 28, Suhaili's obligation on the contract ended.

As they were structuring the Project Varyag down to the last detail, the PLAN lobby never took account of Montreux Convention, and Turkey's sovereignty upon the straits. The PLAN lobby took the project over after it had begun and were maintaining it through Chong Lot. So, when China Shipbuilding Industry, Inc. heard about Xu's unsuccessful application, they probably did nothing but pass this negative situation over to China, to which they were only directed to endeavour towards obtaining an aircraft carrier at every cost, and to persist until the aim was achieved.

The refusal of the second request for transit was an enormous disappointment for both ITC and China. Even though two tugs of ITC remained on the Black Sea as they were paid to be, the wait had gotten bothersome for Joop Timmermans as well. He wanted to see the undertaken job finished as soon as possible, and this was his incontestable right. The contract they signed with Chong Lot, whom they had seen as a commercial enterprise, stated that Varyag's first stop would be Macau. However, rumours that Varyag would not be transformed into a floating entertainment center and casino had travelled all the way to Timmermans and his staff. After discussing it with responsible people in Ankara during the wait, they decided those rumours were indeed true. On one of their usual Istanbul visits, Timmermans had the opportunity to discuss the matter with one of Turkey's biggest holdings' CEO and asked him whether he would be able to find out the underlying reason for the refusal of passage. A few days after that visit, the answer arrived: "I recommend you not to get involved." Apparently, the wait would take longer than expected. Sandy Cape was strong enough to spend the whole winter on the Black Sea along with Varyag. ITC decided to withdraw the tug Sumatras, and on October 27, Sumatras left Sandy Cape alone with Varyag, and set off from Black Sea to Palermo for her new mission.

Both Turkish and global media had begun to get the wind of the circumstances as well. While the national press displayed Turkey's block of the carrier, the global media was also keeping tabs on the situation. China was worried, and rightly so. If the press started investigating, Project Varyag could be unveiled. After five months of deadlock for China, in mid-November, Yao Kuangyi, Chinese Ambassador for Turkey, received an open instruction from the Chinese government to interfere with Varyag's passage through the Bosphorus. Appointed as ambassador in 1997 and speaking fluent Turkish, Yao Kuangyi had previously served as second secretary, first secretary, and consultant, respectively. China wanted the ambassador to do his best to get Varyag through the straits as soon as possible.

Knuckling down immediately upon his instructions, Ambassador Yao's first stop was the Turkish foreign ministry. At that time, diplomatic relations between the Republic of

Turkey and the People's Republic of China went back only 29 years. Between 1949 and 1971, Turkey had recognised "China" as the Republic of China in Taiwan, instead of the People's Republic. The reason behind it was Turkey's implementation of a Chinese policy parallel to the US and Western Europe in the political, economic, military, and diplomatic fields during the period of international political and military tension, namely the Cold War, between 1947-1991 between the Western world led by the US and the communist bloc led by the Soviet Union. Diplomatic relations between Turkey and China were first formed in 1971, when Turkey, along with many other states, ceased to recognise Taiwan upon the United Nations' admission of the People's Republic of China, and afterwards political relations normalised by opening mutual embassies in Ankara and Beijing.

The first high-profile visit between Turkey and China took place in 1985. On June 29, 1985, the visit of then-prime minister Turgut Ozal ensured 400 million dollars of trade agreements. One year later, Chinese Prime Minister Zhao Ziyang made a reciprocal visit. After developing relations through the 1990s, the highest-profile visit took place. In May 1995, President Suleyman Demirel visited China, inviting Jiang Zemin to Turkey. President Jiang Zemin visited in April 2000, one month before Suleyman Demirel's term was due to end. It also happened to be two months before Varyag's departure from Mykolaiv. It was a landmark visit in terms of developing bilateral relations between these two states. President Jiang was welcomed with a formal ceremony at Cankaya Palace in Ankara and was given the Order of Merit of the State, the highest order of Turkey. After attending the banquet given in honour of Prime Minister Bulent Ecevit, President Jiang went on to Istanbul by private plane. President Jiang, and Wang Yeping, his wife, were welcomed at the airport by Suleyman Demirel with a military ceremony. Unaware that Varyag's passage would shortly create a problem between two countries, the two leaders toured the Bosphorus, the heart and soul of the matter, in a boat for longer than an hour, despite the rain and fog.

At the time of this visit, Turkey had a coalition government consisting of Democratic Left Party (DSP), Nationalist Movement Party (MHP), and Motherland Party (ANAP), led by Bulent Ecevit. The longest-lived coalition government of Republic of Turkey's history, the 57th Government had made a statement, "We will make a point of developing our relations with People's Republic of China on various levels," on its political platform. The government's foreign minister, Ismail Cem, had the same duty on both 55th and 56th coalition governments, trying to bring some economical perspective into foreign policy during his continuous triple-term. Upon the formal visit of Ismail Cem, as the Foreign Minister of 55th coalition government, to China within this framework in February 1998, Bulent Ecevit, as the vice-prime minister of the same government also paid a visit to China in May of the same year. Ismail Cem was a member of DSP, formed in the leadership of Bulent Ecevit, and both of them valued Sino-Turkish relations. Therefore, it was only natural that the 57th government programme included this specific statement regarding the development of relations with China. Although at first this seemed like an advantage, the fact that the government was a three-party coalition confused the issue. Maritime Affairs was under direct jurisdiction of Minister Ramazan Mirzaoglu, responsible for naval affairs, from the MHP wing of the government. Coalition partners were not always expected to work in harmony, there were occasional conflicts.

Ambassador Yao learned from the Turkish Foreign Ministry that the carrier was not allowed to pass the Bosphorus due to lack of adequate technical measures for a safe passage. Upon his dialogue with the Foreign Ministry, Yao was not pessimistic, but worried. The diplomatic push he initiated needed to be sustained at higher levels. Indeed, on the first days of 2001, it was planned that Chinese Foreign Minister Tang Jiaxuan would formally visit Turkey. However, before dealing with China's top level diplomatic attempts, it is worth taking a look at how Beijing evaluated those incidents in Turkey.

CHAPTER 5

SWAP

In Beijing, the reason for the blockage was thought to be the US, rather than a technical issue. According to China, the US was trying to block Varyag's passage via NATO ally Turkey. China's assessment was that the US considered Varyag – even if she was incomplete – as an aircraft carrier, and a threat to its regional allies such as Taiwan, South Korea, Japan and so on.

Could the US, after not making a fuss over Soviet-made aircraft carriers, have changed its perspective when it came to its allies in the Pacific? The answer could be found in the reports entitled "Military Power of People's Republic of China", which had been presented to the US Congress every year since 2000 – except 2001, when 9/11 occurred – and dealt with the People's Liberation Army's current and prospective military strategy. Although the possible progress of the Chinese Navy is explained in detail in all of the aforementioned reports, only two of pre-2006 reports (2002 and 2003) mentioned the aircraft carrier, and they used the same sentence: "<u>Aircraft Carrier</u>: While China continues to research and discuss possibilities, it seems like it has forever put aside the purchase of an aircraft carrier."

As it is understood from the reports, despite China being uneasy about US involvement, and US Pacific allies worried about the possibility of the Varyag being converted into an operational aircraft carrier, the US Department of Defense did not deem Varyag worthy of their interest and were practically ignoring her.

At this point, a possible solution to the deadlock seemed to be considered in the confidential discussions between Chinese top level military officials. Although never officially confirmed (and surely never will be), it ought to be considered here. The basis for this possible solution arose from an international aviation accident, and the diplomatic tension that formed in the aftermath between Washington and Beijing.

This accident took place on Sunday, April 1, 2001, at 9:07 AM, in the South China Sea, approximately 65 miles southeast of Hainan, the biggest Chinese island. A US Navy EP-3 reconnaissance aircraft with a crew of 24, had a mid-air collision with PRC's J-8 naval warplane. The damaged American plane made an emergency landing on the Lingshui military airport of Hainan Island, while the Chinese warplane crash-landed into the sea, and the pilot Wang Wei went missing. Sino-American relations had already suffered grave effects from the Taiwan Strait Crisis and the bombing of the Chinese Embassy in Belgrade. This crash would light the fuse of a new crisis, that could be seen as the third of the series.

U.S. Navy EP-3 Electronic reconnaissance aircraft. *Photo by U.S. Navy.*

Thirteen hours after the accident, a statement was made by the Chinese Ministry of Foreign Affairs on state television: "An American plane violating Chinese airspace 'suddenly' veered towards the Chinese plane, which had been on a routine flight, crashing it with her nose and her left wing, causing her to crash." Only a few hours later, Admiral Dennis Blair, Commander of the U.S. Pacific Command, declared in a press statement in Hawaii that the EP-3 surveillance aircraft was on a "routine operation" in international airspace over the South China Sea about 70 miles off Hainan island, when it was intercepted by PLA fighters, and one of them "bumped into the wing of the EP-3E aircraft." Reporting that the pilot had made a mayday call, and an emergency landing on Hainan, Blair also stressed that the plane had "sovereign immunity", and that China could not board, seize, or inspect her. That evening, Assistant of Chinese Ministry of Foreign Affairs Zhou Wenzhong summoned Joseph Prueher, US Ambassador for China, to the ministry, in protest. The next meeting between the two would be about 24 hours later. At that time, Zhou demanded the US take full responsibility for the incident and apologise to the Chinese government and people.

The US administration was led by George W. Bush, who had won the presidency little more than two months before. They were facing their first big crisis in foreign policy. Since the parties had different claims about the basic cause of the accident, it did not seem likely that they would agree about when and how the US crew and plane would be released, whether the US government would apologise, or whether China had the right to get on board and make inspections on the plane.

Discontented with Beijing's demeanour, the Washington administration was worried that the plane could be held for a long time, along with the crew. On April 2, after a National Security Council meeting, President Bush made a public statement that their priority was for both the crew's and the plane's safe return, as soon as possible. He further indicated he was troubled that China was not allowing US embassy staff to contact the US flight crew.

With this declaration, Bush carried the crisis to the level of national leadership. President Jiang Zemin also did not stand idle, and the next day demanded the US take full responsibility and stop reconnaissance flights. That night, in the midst of these negative developments, Neal Sealock, US Senior Defense Attaché at US Embassy Beijing found a chance to contact the crew, despite not being able to also set them free. Getting information about the crew from Sealock, Bush made a second statement, declaring that hopes for building good relations between the two countries could be damaged, and emphasized that "It is now time" to release the crew and the plane. In return, President Jiang made a declaration on April 4, before setting out to visit six Latin America countries, inviting the USA to "apologise" for the accident. The same day, Tang Jiaxuan, Chinese Minister of Foreign Affairs, summoned Ambassador Prueher to his office, declaring loudly and clearly that if the US admitted their fault and apologised, the crew would be released.

The message was received. Secretary of State Colin Powell sent a letter to Vice-President Qian Qichen via the US Ambassador, not apologising but stating his sorrow for the missing Chinese pilot and the crashed Chinese plane. This was the first step toward changing the course of the crisis, but it was not deemed sufficient. China was expecting an official apology.

With that, a similar declaration came on April 5 from President Bush. In his third statement, Bush also expressed his sorrow, sent his prayers for the pilot, pilot's family, and the crew, adding, "We should not let this incident upset our relations." In Chile, his first stop in Latin America, Jiang insisted on the apology, but also remarked that they could work for a solution to help bilateral relations, in a reconciliatory manner. Upon the leaders' positive messages, long days of tension gave way to some serenity, leading to a solution by diplomacy.

SWAP

Negotiations began almost immediately, with the main agenda being, as might be expected, the "apology" China requested in every statement. A few days of hard bargains paved the way to reconciliation and on April 11, US Ambassador Joseph Prueher presented to the Minister of Foreign Affairs Tang Jiaxuan a letter in English. A retired admiral, Ambassador Prueher stated in his carefully penned post, "Both President Bush and Secretary of State Powell have expressed their sincere regret over your missing pilot and aircraft. Please convey to the Chinese people and to the family of pilot Wang Wei that we are very sorry for their loss," before adding, "We are very sorry the entering of China's airspace and the landing did not have verbal clearance, but very pleased the crew landed safely." China's expectation was met. Tang said he accepted the letter, and China announced they would let the US crew – out of humanitarian considerations – leave China. But how could that letter without even one mention of the word "apology" be accepted by China, despite all those previous insistent demands?

In truth, this question has only one answer. Now known as "The Letter of Two Sorries" in diplomatic history, that script was a masterpiece of wording and linguistics. "Very sorry" in the letter corresponded to "deep apology" in Chinese. The US had avoided using the word "apology" since the day of the accident, instead preferring "regret". After China insisted on the word "sorry", the word took part in the letter. Only with one difference – adding "very" before it.

In this way, both sides had gotten what they wanted. On the early morning of April 12, the US crew left China. Despite the plane's return being still problematic, the crisis had ended.

After the EP-3 crew came back safe and sound, negotiations began between the US and China for the plane's return. Upon reaching an agreement, the logistics of EP-3's return became an issue of priority. The simplest, fastest, and cheapest way to do it was repair on site and then leave under its own power; however, China saw that the aircraft's possible self-powered departure from Hainan would be felt as a "national humiliation", after she had caused the loss of both a Chinese pilot and warplane. There was no other transporting option than deconstruction. China agreed to the offer of transportation via a third country's cargo plane. Thereupon, the EP-3 was deconstructed by American technicians, and then its fuselage and other parts were loaded onto a Russian Antonov-124 type giant cargo plane. Flown by Russian crew, the cargo plane departed from Hainan on July 3, and stopped off in Manila, Philippines, and Hickam Air Force Base at Hawaii for fuel charge, until finally landing in Dobbins Air Base in the state of Georgia on July 5.

After seeing this accident and its aftermath discussed in detail, the allegation regarding its role in the Varyag affair is more or less obvious: the EP-3 was released to ensure the release of the Varyag. It was thought to be the basis for a swap of interests. The biggest basis for that is shown that during the negotiations regarding the EP-3's return, China made a demand from the USA "to convince Turkey to let Varyag pass through Turkish Straits" and may have got assurance for it. The only evidence to support this allegation is that these negotiations were also being conducted with officials of the People's Liberation Army in Beijing.

The admission of this allegation leads to a suspicion as well: Was the EP-3's landing in Hainan, in one way or another, desired by Chinese naval officials right from the beginning? Because it is not a secret that since the 1950s, the US army had been making reconnaissance flights all around the world, including Chinese coasts. During these flights, blocking attempts – forcing planes to change routes – by other parties' warplanes, usually two of them, is seen as quite normal by the Pentagon. Indeed, many such "blocks" between Russian and American aircrafts have been recorded. But some things within Chinese airspace had also changed in the last months of 2000.

According to the Pentagon, Chinese aircrafts had begun to make unorthodox aggressive blocks since mid-December 2000.

These blocks were made within risky distances between planes, near the southern coasts of China, including the day of the crash; of the forty-four blocks, six of them had occurred as close as 30 feet, and two of them as close as 10 feet. This belligerent attitude of China regarding reconnaissance flights suggests a few scenarios; the most likely one among them is that the US increased the frequency of their reconnaissance flights, and China reacted harder than expected.

The other scenario which could coincide with the aforementioned suspicion is that the naval pilots such as Wang Wei in Hainan took individual risks – Top Gun style. It remains unknown whether Wang Wei had received an order to force the reconnaissance aircraft to land. These aggressive blocks within Chinese airspaces seemed to begin immediately after China launched their diplomatic attack to get Varyag through Turkish Straits.

Assuming for the moment that there was a connection, would the US have approved such a swap? It is incredibly unlikely that the US would give up on an aircraft worth 80 million dollars, which held assorted surveillance equipment and intelligence data. But even if that was the case, would it be correct to label this as a swap?

EP-3's departure from Hainan was in July 2001, whereas Varyag's passage through Turkish Straits took place months later. Could a swap hold good when one party received their share early, on the strength of a mere promise? Moreover, could a promise be valid when it involved persuasion of a third party?

Despite the US and Turkey being NATO allies, it was impossible for the US to ask Turkey to "permit or not" Varyag's passage through Turkish Straits, where Turkey has sovereignty and holds great sensitivity regarding it. To show an example of that sensitivity towards the straits, it would be worth mentioning briefly how Turkey did not let US naval ships pass in 2008.

VARYAG

After the conflicts between Russia and Georgia in August 2008, known as the South-Ossetia War or Russo-Georgian War, the US planned to send two hospital ships to Georgia, USN Comfort and USN Mercy, which in total weighed nearly 140 thousand tons, for humanitarian aid purposes. Turkey did not grant the request for these ships to pass to the Black Sea, citing the Montreux Convention. Upon meeting this refusal, the US overcame this problem by sending ships with lower tonnage.

But was there no communication between the US and Turkey about Varyag? There most definitely was, it should not be possible to think otherwise! However, it could be said that the scope of this communication did not go further than simply "briefing." That is to say, it is rumoured that in the NATO meetings between military delegations, the US informed Turkey that Varyag could be studied and reproduced by China and that this could upset Taiwan, South Korea, and Japan.

In the end, the idea that there was a swap was only based in China's negative perception of the US as the central and controlling obstacle in Varyag's way. For China, to ask the US to convince Turkey meant asking the US to "get out of the way". But one thing China did not know was that the US was never in the way. If the allegation of a quid pro quo swap was true, the USA had seen through China's perceptions, played their part well, and had gotten their aircraft by approving a swap without losing anything on their end.

Since Beijing's perception of the incidents in Turkey has been relayed, it is time to take a look at what went on during the diplomatic contacts started by Ambassador Yao taken under the Chinese administration's directive, and advanced during Minister of Foreign Affairs Tang Jiaxuan's visit in January 2001.

CHAPTER 6

THE GREAT GAME

"You cannot witness the strait anywhere else but in Istanbul." Xu Kun, Chinese Consulate-General in Istanbul, said this in a program broadcast on Chinese Radio International (CRI), about the Bosphorus. He must have expressed a similar view when he was accompanying Chinese Foreign Minister Tang Jiaxuan on the minister's visit to Istanbul's historical and touristic spots. The minister had arrived in Istanbul on Saturday, January 6, 2001, on his way to handle his official agenda in Ankara. Then he was met at the airport by Governor of Istanbul Erol Cakir and Consulate-General Xu Kun. There would be a set of meetings between the two countries' delegations, and they would be led by the foreign ministers. Turkey's Ministry of Foreign Affairs declared that the meetings would make a point of exploring opportunities to develop bilateral relations between Turkey and China and to consult each other regarding international matters.

After his Istanbul visit and a day-long Izmir visit, Chinese Foreign Minister Tang traveled to Ankara. He was welcomed in Cankaya Mansion by President Necdet Sezer, who had assumed his duties in May 2000 from Suleyman Demirel. Welcomed also by Prime Minister Bulent Ecevit the same day, Tang later met with Foreign Minister Ismail Cem. After the inter-delegation meetings were held in the House of Foreign Affairs, the ministers signed an action plan for developing relations between the two countries in various fields before holding a joint press conference. Cem stated that the growing accordance between Turkey and China, with mutual respect, had taken a more concrete shape with the signing of an action plan. Tang followed this by expressing that this action plan would serve to build the Silk Road of the 21st century between Turkey and China.

It was quite significant that they did not speak of the Varyag issue during either the visits or the statements afterward. Instead, they preferred the more usual discourse of diplomatic custom that usually followed bilateral discussions and agreements of this kind. It seemed as if the issue of the giant carrier never came to the fore. However, a few months later, these words uttered by Ismail Cem at the joint press conference would be associated with Varyag: "There will be endeavours to canalise some of the 180 million Chinese tourists visiting abroad Turkey."

Exactly twelve years after this visit, Southern Weekly, considered the most outspoken paper in China, published an article titled "The Secrets of Varyag's Journey to China" by Ye Biao. This piece shed light on those days, featuring an interview with Yao Kuangyi, who had been China's Ambassador for Ankara and Director of East Asia and North Africa Department. With Ambassador Yao's memoirs, the interview mentioned that Tang, after meeting with Ecevit and Cem, "stated (to both the PM and the foreign minister) that China wishes the carrier to be released, yet the PM seemed rather ambiguous, while the minister of foreign affairs was more positive."

Although the Foreign Minister Tang's visit to Turkey did not solve the problem, it did accelerate the process. Indeed, Ambassador Yao, responsible for managing the trip, would ever continue his determined attempts. Touted as "the envoy of Varyag" by the writer Ye Biao, Yao also mentioned in his memoirs his meeting with Maritime Affairs Minister Prof. Dr. Ramazan Mirzaoglu,. Mirzaoglu was elected as a deputy of MHP from Kirsehir while acting as the Dean of the Faculty of Science and Letters. Afterward, he was appointed as a minister of the state within the 57th Cabinet. Yao had visited Mirzaoglu,

THE GREAT GAME

whom he saw as the highest-ranked official then available to release Varyag, after Tang left Turkey. At this meeting, Mirzaoglu had stated that a safe passage was not possible, elaborating on the reasons in detail. He recommended two methods for Varyag's passage: The first involved towing Varyag back to the Ukrainian shipyard and getting a power system and steering installed (thus allowing her to move on her own). The second option was dividing her into two.

Mirzaoglu gave great importance to the security of Turkish Straits. To this end, he developed and realized the project "Turkish Straits Vessel Traffic Management and Information System," which is one of his most significant acts as a minister and still in operation. Its aim was to provide fairway security on Bosphorus and Dardanelles. It was initiated by the maritime affairs minister just a few weeks before Yao's visit, at a ceremony held in Istinye on the European side of Istanbul. Actually, the first actions regarding this project were taken in the early 90s. However, even though the Turkish Maritime Organization had twice invited bids, the situation remained inconclusive. After a Council of Minister's decision in 1996, even the Undersecretariat of Maritime Affairs was drawn into inviting bids. Yet this tender was also canceled, after the conditions of the competition were not met.

The next tender was offered in 1999 during the approximately five-month-long 56th Cabinet when Bulent Ecevit served as the prime minister. It was concluded during the 57th Cabinet with Mirzaoglu's ministry. The tender was won by the famous defense industry company Lockheed Martin from the US. After negotiations, the contract with them was signed in February 2000. The computer-aided project was based on the provision of radar, satellite control, meteorological and oceanographic detectors, a day and night camera surveillance system, and communication equipment, supported by 13 traffic monitoring stations – 8 on Bosphorus, 5 on Dardanelles – and two separate control centers in Istanbul and Canakkale. After the commence of the system's operational service on December 30, 2003, passage through the Turkish Straits, two of the world's busiest and – in regard to cruising hardships – riskiest waterways, were now provided with more safety.

Coming back to Yao, it would not be possible to say that he was satisfied with his meeting with Mirzaoglu. Like Beijing, Yao also considered that the main factor behind Varyag being disallowed passage through the straits, was for security reasons, from the US position. Indeed, this opinion led to Yao holding a rather unexpected meeting. To ascertain their point of view, he met Robert Pearson, U.S. Ambassador to Turkey (served 2000-2003). Although Yao managed to mention the project undertaken by American company Lockheed Martin, he failed to raise the issue of Varyag directly and came out empty-handed.

While, according to Yao's account, these movements were happening on Varyag's side, Turkey was gradually heading towards the biggest economic crisis of the Republican Era. In the early 2000s, Turkey was running an economic program based on "free-floating interest, free-floating foreign currency" supported by IMF's lower high-soaring inflation. However, in November 2000, the liquidity crisis broke out and interest rates sharply rose. After the Central Bank funded the markets with IMF support, despite the interest rates remaining high, markets were at that time provided with relief. This shallow relief came to an end at the National Security Council (MGK) meeting on February 19, 2001.

A few days before this meeting, President Necdet Sezer instructed the State Inspection Council (DDK) to inspect public banks regarding "non-performing loans." At the MGK meeting held in Cankaya Mansion, during a quarrel between them about the inspection, Sezer threw a constitutional code booklet at Ecevit, and the PM reacted by leaving the meeting. Upon his declaration to the journalists waiting outside that this was "a government crisis," the precarious tight-rope economic balance was lost. The stock market slumped, and interest rates spiked

THE GREAT GAME

up. As such, a crisis summit was held immediately, resulting in a decision to switch to a floating rate policy. The Turkish Lira lost approximately fifty percent of its value. This major crisis had not only economic but also political consequences. It was fueled by the quarrels at the level of the head of government, informed by a high budgetary deficit and with public debt having become unsustainable.

Right after the incident, Ecevit invited Kemal Dervis – then First Vice-President of the World Bank – to Ankara. The day after his arrival, Dervis was appointed as the Minister of Economic Affairs. Taking part in the cabinet as the sole nonpartisan minister, Dervis prepared the "Transition to Strong Economy Programme," that aimed to elude the crisis environment, fight inflation, and provide sustainable growth, which was put into effect in April 2001. Along with World Bank credits, the stand-by arrangement signed with the IMF supported the program,. And yet, stand-by meant "bitter medicine" for Turkish people. Despite this, there were signs of recovery in economic indicators in 2002 that were attributable to the program. However, people did not show mercy after the troublesome crisis, and the general elections in November 2002 exacted a toll on the members of the coalition government of the 1999-2002 era – DSP, MHP, and ANAP. After this election, these parties were left under the electoral threshold.

The financial crisis in Turkey hindered the wheels of the economy, but diplomatic and bureaucratic processes carried on. So did, of course, Ambassador Yao's endeavors. After the crisis broke out, one of the first names he visited was Suat Caglayan, then Turkish Grand National Assembly (TBMM) Foreign Affairs Commission Deputy President and a Deputy of DSP. As Caglayan also expressed afterward, the goal of Yao's visit was, obviously, getting help for Varyag's passage through the straits. When Yao informed him about Varyag's situation and the Undersecretariat of Maritime Affairs' demeanor, Suat Caglayan inevitably found himself involved due to his position within the commission. He communicated with the Foreign

Ministry before and with the Maritime Undersecretariat after the meeting. Foreign Ministry said that, based on the Montreux Convention, there was no obstacle in the way for Varyag, as she stood. The Maritime Undersecretariat, their negative stance about the matter known, claimed "security" as the reason for their attitude. However, the meeting with Suat Caglayan revealed a different side of the case.

An anonymous senior official that Caglayan met in private said or blurted out that, while the security of the straits was important, but that the ministry to which the Undersecretariat of Maritime Affairs reports, and therefore Minister Ramazan Mirzaoglu, saw China's oppression of Uyghur Turks as more critical. Combining his knowledge from the ministry and the undersecretariat with what he learned from the ambassador, Caglayan concluded that Minister Ramazan Mirzaoglu still wished to block China from having the carrier.

According to Suat Caglayan, Mirzaoglu, a member of MHP, was surely acting by his own worldview. However, as a deputy belonging to the coalition's DSP wing, Caglayan opined that Varyag's passage should be allowed, as long as it stayed within international regulations. He wasted no time acting, and obtained an appointment from PM Ecevit, informing him of the situation. Ecevit attentively listened to Caglayan without making comments, then said, "I requested the minister to allow this carrier to pass. Let's wait." When Yao heard the PM's words from Caglayan, whom he visited weekly, he began to hope more strongly. How could he not? The PM's positive approach was not enough by itself. But the carrier could never make her passage without his approval, either. But this mention of Uyghur Turks was bothersome as for the Chinese side.

Uyghur Turks are a Muslim ethnic group residing for centuries in northwest China within Xinjiang Uyghur Autonomous Region, which has the largest surface area among Chinese province-level divisions but the least dense population. Once a tribe connected with Gokturk Khaganate, they remained in later periods – apart from short-term independence – under

Chinese domination. After the Qing Dynasty established the Xinjiang region in 1884, Uyghurs were subjugated by the Republic of China in 1912 and People's Republic of China in 1949. This incident was followed by the First East Turkistan Republic (1933-1934) from independence movements, and the Second East Turkistan Republic (1944-1949) with Soviet Union's support. However, the existence of both states ceased after Chinese army invasions. In 1955, Xinjiang's status as a province was changed into an autonomous region. Since Uyghur Turks never renounced their bid for independence, China's prevailing perception of the threat towards Xinjiang became even stronger after the Soviet Union's collapse, as the Turkic republics of Middle Asia declared independence.

Seeking to improve its dominance within this region with its rich underground and surface resources, China formed a new population policy. After altering the region's demographic structure with these policies from 1949 onwards, the "Go to West!" campaign was initiated, aiming to end the Uyghurs' population majority. This campaign resulted in the Han population – the largest ethnic group in China – spiking up from around 10% in 1949 to 40% in 2000 in these remote lands.

China justified this campaign as "the aim to channel domestic and foreign investments to Xinjiang and neighboring Tibet Autonomous Regions and develop these regions". However, many analysts stated that they did not find this campaign trustworthy. According to these assessments, China was only trying to alter the demographic structure to more easily command and exploit natural resources. During the early years of the 21st century, the situation in Xinjiang was relatively calm, though the period for Varyag to pass through Turkish Straits had been just after the beginning of the "Go to West!" campaign.

At the time of this writing, it has been twenty-one years since Varyag passed through the Turkish Straits. Maintaining his nationalist perspective, Mirzaoglu still attempts to make

Uyghur Turks heard via his Twitter posts. However, he is no longer an active politician. However, he never uttered a word about Chinese policy toward Uyghur Turks in his press statements during his ministry and regarding Varyag afterward. Apparently, the association between Uyghur Turks and Varyag was no more than a false assumption by that top undersecretariat official.

The Turkish authorities' decision to deny Varyag's passage through the Turkish Straits was made under the pretext of avoiding an unsafe journey. It became increasingly clear that this decision was not motivated by a US request to safeguard its allies in the Asia-Pacific region nor for Mirzaoglu's position, which was related to China's pressure on the Uyghur Turks. Well then, since both claims are proven wrong, could it be said that there were no other factors around the secure passage justification? We cannot easily say "yes," as we can talk about two factors that support the "secure passage" justification. Since these two issues of the 90s, "Turkish Straits Regulations" and "transporting Caspian oil to world markets," were interrelated, they should be assessed together. In this way, it may be possible to identify what is the main factor behind the rationale for "safe passage" and even its main objective, if such exists.

The Turkish Straits Maritime Traffic Order Regulations, which Turkey prepared to maintain the safety of life, property, environment, and cruise on Turkish Straits, came into effect in July 1994. However, beginning from the very first day of their practice, the International Maritime Organization received criticism regarding these regulations from countries that used the straits often, especially Russia, and for political and economic concerns rather than technical reasons. There was an attempt to create an international popular opinion about this. However, Turkey voiced at IMO meetings that this was solely a technical matter. Accordingly, in 1998, new regulations with necessary adaptations and alterations were implemented in line with four-year experiences of practice. Ultimately, at the 71st term meeting of the Maritime Safety Committee in 1999, the recommendation made by the working group on this matter to remove it from the IMO agenda was approved, and then, at the 21st General Assembly, this recommendation was adopted. This development was seen as a declaration that the legal rules Turkey laid down for Turkish Straits' security were in accordance with international rules and law. This strengthened Turkey's hand.

The main reason behind Russia's disturbance regarding the Straits Regulations and political struggle against Turkey was that some of these regulations would affect the passage of ships carrying oil and other hazardous material through the straits. Russia was bringing a substantial amount of the oil they produced themselves and the oil they bought cheap from former Soviet states around Caspian Sea, via pipelines or railway, to start voyages from Black Sea harbors. These were then transported on tankers through Turkish Straits to world markets, beginning with Europe. Turkey's limitation of the passage of giant oil tankers through straits could lead to delayed passages that were not acceptable to Russia. The country's economic improvement was based mostly on oil and gas exports after the dissolution of the Soviet Union. If regulations remained in force, it would restrict oil export and their power on international competition. However, a significant decline could be obtained in the number of accidents on the straits after the passage of ships was regulated and disciplined by certain rules. It would be unthinkable that Turkey would primarily bother itself with Russia's possible reduction of oil export revenue. On top of this, the Straits Regulations were being discussed as a new model of how and through which routes that Caspian oil, the center of global and regional powers' attention after the dissolution of the Soviets, would be transported to world markets. Russia and Turkey were in a tight race for this.

Above all, Azerbaijan, Kazakhstan, and Turkmenistan, all newly independent and coastal states of the Caspian Sea, needed to use the rich oil and gas sources they had on and around the Caspian Sea to rebuild their economy in the post-independence era, just like Russia. In fact, Azerbaijan had already embarked on this quest before they won their independence, when the cracks in the Soviet system emerged. Desiring independence from Russia in the oil industry yet seeing they could not succeed on their own either, Azerbaijan took its first concrete step in 1990. Kaspmorneftegas, the state's open sea oil company, made an agreement with Scottish Ramco Energy to listen closely to Europe and find investment partners. This was followed in 1991 by a tender for the rights to drill in the Azerbaijani oil field, which was 62 miles east of Baku on Caspian Sea, and the same year in June, American company Amoco won the bidding. After the result, Amoco signed an AMI (Area of Mutual Interest) contract with Ramco and other Western companies that also made bids – BP (United Kingdom), Unocal (US), McDermott (US), and Statoil (Norway) – to work jointly on the Azerbaijani field. This enterprise should have stemmed from Azerbaijan's need to be supported by the companies' home countries. This was a strategy for finding a sense of security after the years of constant Russian pressure. However, this progress on the eve of independence was hindered when minor clashes between Azerbaijan and Armenia, ongoing intermittently since 1988, turned into hot conflict after both countries gained independence. The reason for the clashes was that Armenians living in the Nagorno-Karabakh Autonomous Oblast wanted the region transferred from Azerbaijan to Armenia. While the clashes continued, Azerbaijan had its first democratic elections in June 1992. Abulfaz Elchibey, who led a civil movement that identified as anti-Soviet during the dissolution of the USSR, would then institutionalize under the name Azerbaijani Popular Front, and it received 60% of the vote in presidential elections. At the beginning of his work, Elchibey was determined to resume negotiations with Western oil companies on the condition that Turkey would also sit at the table.

With some distance from Russia and the Commonwealth of Independent States (CIS) led by Russia, Elchibey made it his foreign policy priority to get close to Turkey, which shares similar values to his nation. He made his first foreign visit to Turkey just after he won the election, within a very short time, in his first two weeks. His admiration for Mustafa Kemal Ataturk, the founder of Turkey known, Elchibey made a speech at the Grand National Assembly with his emphatic Azerbaijani Turkish. In that, he mentioned that during his fighting years for independence, when he was asked, "What will you do?" he replied: "Our way is firstly Mustafa Kemal's way, and then we will find our state." The same year, at the end of October, along with presidents of former-Soviet nations Kazakhstan, Kyrgyzstan, Uzbekistan, and Turkmenistan, Elchibey attended the first Turkic Speaking States Summit hosted by Turkish President Turgut Ozal, with whom he visited various Turkish cities after the summit. His visit to Izmir took off with an official ceremony and an enthusiastic greeting. In the evening hours, he met Ozal privately in his hotel room, asking Turkey to take part as well in the deals with Western oil companies. Ozal saw this as an unmissable opportunity for Turkey, and that very night, he sent the experts of Turkish Petroleum Corporation (TPAO) and Petroleum Pipeline Corporation (BOTAS) to Azerbaijan. TPAO would be included in oil exploration and drilling deals, while BOTAS would get involved in the pipeline working group. Upon arriving at Baku, those experts contacted the State Oil Company of Azerbaijan Republic (SOCAR), which was founded with Elchibey's order, and the other companies that signed the AMI contract, to manage and assess the oil and gas resources of the country. In early November, five memorandums of understanding regarding cooperation in the oil business were signed between SOCAR and foreign oil companies, including Turkish ones. This development meant that Turkey would find itself in the big oil game. Although Western oil companies were not quite pleased with Turkish involvement, everything developed

VARYAG

rapidly for Turkey, at least in the beginning. So much so that, just a few months later, in March 1993 in Ankara, an international contract was signed between Hikmet Cetin, Foreign Minister of Turkey, and Sabit Bagirov, Elchibey's Advisor on Strategic Programmes, also Chairman of SOCAR. This contract included a pipeline installation between Baku and Ceyhan (a district on Turkey's Mediterranean shore) transporting the oil Azerbaijan – not having any shores on open seas – will produce to Ceyhan through Turkish lands.

Despite its fast-paced beginning, however, the process did not advance as expected. Towards the end of March, Armenian forces attacked. They seized Azerbaijan's Kalbajar district, which served as a corridor between Armenia and Nagorno-Karabakh. In early April, during the fall of Kalbajar, friendly nation Turkey was keeping a worried eye on the situation. However, President Turgut Ozal and PM Suleyman Demirel were split in opinion about the manner of support that could be given to Azerbaijan. This was yet another in a long-standing series of clashes of authority between the two branches of Turkish executive power. Ozal insisted that Turkey should side with Azerbaijan and intervene against Armenian aggression. Indeed, he also wanted to make a military intervention in the Mosul-Kirkuk oil region during the Gulf War of 1991, seeing an opportunity after the US intervened against the Saddam regime. But he could not convince the army – despite the green light to this venture from the US – and after Chief of General Staff Necip Torumtay resigned, Ozal's project ended fruitless.

Unlike Ozal's American-style proactive approach, Demirel argued for diplomatic solutions. Being the near-future prospective replacement of Ozal, he asserted that Turkey should carry on with their efforts within the Minsk Group, which was formed by Organization for Security and Co-operation in Europe (OSCE) in 1992 to find a peaceful solution to the Nagorno-Karabakh problem between Azerbaijan and Armenia. Being experienced statesmen, Ozal and Demirel, were both aware that Elchibey's policy was not in accordance with Russia's interests, who saw Azerbaijan, along with other former-Soviet nations, as their back garden. Demirel's caution matched Ozal's rashness. Demirel was keeping in mind that Turkey could face Russia, in the event of taking military measures towards Armenia, who had adopted a Russia-centric foreign policy. The day after the occupation of Kalbajar, Turgut Ozal decided to go on a Middle Asia trip consisting of all the countries in Turkic Speaking States Summit, to express his position clearly.

In April 1993, Azerbaijan was the last stop of a ten-day-long visit. Herein, Ozal openly revealed one of the reasons for his trip by stating, "Turkey stood with Azerbaijan, and the patience of Turkish people should not be tried." This tension at the top of the government was expected to heighten, but another development changed everything. Turgut Ozal died of a heart attack in the Presidential Palace on April 17, 1993, only two days after returning from his intense and tiresome trip to Turkic nations. After this incident, claims about his death being an assassination by poison were circulated by family members and his inner political circle. These claims would have continued for many years, and Ozal's grave was opened for an investigation nineteen years after his death. But nothing could be proven definitively. The Turkish Grand National Assembly elected Suleyman Demirel as president in Ozal's stead, as a candidate who had served as prime minister in seven non-consecutive terms.

The sudden death of Turgut Ozal was the first breaking point in Azerbaijani oil's future across Turkish soil. Another arrived with SOCAR's announcement of "Declaration of Use," and included that Chirag and Gunashli oil fields would be drilled along with the Azeri field, which, the foreign companies also concurred on.

However, it escalated when Surat Huseynov, who had been a regiment commander in Ganja, Azerbaijan, led a revolt there. Huseynov had drove his troops towards Baku. Elchibey wanted to eliminate the civil war threat within the country and stepped down from the presidency. Suret Huseynov was, in fact, personally dismissed by Elchibey for his military failure that had led to the loss of settlements around Karabakh. He later flourished after the Russian troops completely withdrew from the country, as this withdrawal left Russian weapons and equipment in his hands, instead of the Azerbaijani army. However, as a result of the actions of the Elchibey administration, the pro-Russian Huseynov's next step was to start a rebellion. This revolt caused not only Elchibey to leave his duty, but also the chairman of the Azerbaijan Supreme Soviet – the parliament of the period – and then the prime minister had to resign. Before Elchibey left Baku to settle in the Autonomous Republic of Nakhchivan, he invited the only person who could provide security and stability in the country, Chairman of Nakhchivan Supreme Assembly Heydar Aliyev to Baku. In this way, the course of events had shifted.

Aliyev had risen to the general rank in KGB and ruled Azerbaijan from 1969 to 1982 as the First Secretary of the Central Committee of the Azerbaijan Communist Party. He was elected to Politburo membership of the Central Committee of the Soviet Union Communist Party after the end of his secretarial duty. Besides, Aliyev was also appointed as First Deputy Chairman of the USSR Council of Ministers. He was forced to resign after differing with Gorbachev's policies. Three years after leaving these duties, he left Moscow. He returned first to Baku, and then his birthplace, Nakhchivan. He resigned his Soviet Union Communist Party membership.

After an invitation to Baku, he was elected to the vacant Azerbaijan Supreme Soviet chairmanship on June 15, 1993. One of Aliyev's first actions was appointing Huseynov as prime minister. Aliyev was a very experienced statesman and knew that Moscow was key to rectifying the situation for his country. It was obvious that Russia could not tolerate being left out of oil deals regarding Azerbaijan. Moreover, this was just after his leaving Politburo membership (i.e., his voice within Soviet Union administration). Armenians of the region

THE GREAT GAME

embarked on separatist actions to create the Nagorno-Karabakh problem, and Russia played with both Azerbaijan and Armenia despite seeming like an impartial mediator. At the same time, Huseynov had Moscow's support – Aliyev could not easily overlook any of these factors. He held Huseynov close in order to control him and strengthen the army. At the same time, to reduce Russia's dissatisfaction, Aliyev wasted no time putting all of the signed oil deals on hold. This development also caused the Baku-Ceyhan pipeline contract to be suspended indefinitely between Azerbaijan and Turkey. Another move by Aliyev was going to Moscow and, as an indication of change, signing the papers for Azerbaijan's participation in CIS – a move which Elchibey had opposed. However, the main expectation of Russia was met after Aliyev received nearly all the votes in the next general election in October of the same year (1993), becoming the president. Russia's biggest oil production company Lukoil was also involved in those oil deals which were on hold, although, most probably it would be reactivated. If that happened, Lukoil would receive a cut-off of SOCAR's share, which corresponded to 10% of all the shares. Actually, it is not possible to say that this gesture satisfied Moscow's expectations entirely. However, Aliyev had at least, shown that he would follow a balanced policy, and the dust settled for a while. Indeed, a protocol mediated by Russia was signed between Azerbaijan and Armenia in Bishkek in May 1994. As such, the ceasefire was declared. Now, the big oil game could resume.

On September 20, 1994, the agreement between SOCAR and the Azerbaijan International Operating Company (AIOC) – a consortium that prominent global oil companies BP, Amoco, Lukoil, Pennzoil (USA), Unocal, Statoil, McDermott, Ramco, TPAO and Delta-Nimir (Saudi Arabia) formed together – was signed regarding the production and sharing of the oil in Azeri-Chirag-Gunashli fields. However, just as on every previous step Azerbaijan took towards oil, this one was also inevitably subjected to undermining interference. Thinking that Aliyev had only come to power thanks to the rebellion that he had led, Huseyinov could not digest the fact that he was being denied the opportunity to participate in a deal resulting from that revolution, worth billions of dollars. For this reason, he again attempted a coup against Aliyev with the support of those troops loyal to him, and at a time when he was Prime Minister of the country, but this time he failed. Fleeing to Moscow afterward, Huseynov was extradited to Azerbaijan a few years later, stood on trial for treason, and was sentenced to life in prison.

The deal was deemed the "Deal of the Century", and would be valid for thirty years. Its first stage was the export of early-production oil, spurting out under its own pressure, before the main production oil aimed to be drilled in the 2000s. Choosing the route and construction of the main export pipeline for the oil produced in this manner would take a long time. So, there were studies about the competing routes to be used for transportation to world markets. Among alternatives, two separate pipeline routes made the cut, possibly reaching out at portal cities Novorossiysk, Russia, and Supsa, Georgia. Besides these, the Baku-Novorossiysk and Baku-Supsa routes were among the four main export pipeline alternatives that were mostly considered and discussed. Other alternatives were Baku-Persian Gulf, which was unlikely to be used because of the ongoing US embargo on Iran since 1979, and, as might be expected, Baku-Ceyhan. When it came to choosing the route for early-production oil, even though Russia shined as the most advantageous country, others made their case. Western countries were operating in the Caspian region via the oil companies of the consortium. These rivals could not possibly overlook Russia's threat of monopoly, thanks to their existing pipelines built on their own soil from the Soviet Union. This was the physical advantage that gave a remaining influence over former-Soviet countries. To counter this, Western countries led by the US adopted a strategy called "multiple pipelines." They argued that early-production oil should be transported through both Baku-Novorossiysk and Baku-Suspa routes instead of just one route. In that vein, Turkey did not abstain from supporting the Baku-Suspa route to override the rival Baku-Novorossiysk line, and to increase their chance of becoming the main route. The rivalry between the great powers manifested itself from the very beginning. Heydar Aliyev decided to transport the early oil through two separate pipelines in order to maintain his policy of balance. Although this method was not economical, it allowed Aliyev to avoid confronting Russia while meeting the demand of Western countries. In 1996, SOCAR and AIOC signed the first agreements with Transneft, the pipeline transportation company owned by the Russian state. The second agreement was with the Georgian government concerning the transportation of early-production oil. The Baku-Novorossiysk pipeline, installed in 1983 and used in the transportation of Russian crude oil, entered into service in 1997 after being operated in reverse with the reparation and renovation on some parts. In contrast, the construction of the Baku-Supsa pipeline began the same year, to be completed in 1999.

Actually, Turkey had taken a great risk by supporting the Baku-Supsa route. If the capacity of the line Turkey supports for transporting early-production oil was increased, there could be a possibility for it to turn into the main export pipeline. In that case, the Supsa line would be no different from the Novorossiysk line. Elchibey and Ozal had set forth a vision of exporting Azerbaijani oil through Turkish territory. Turkey's ambition was to make this vision a reality. This ambition was not only rooted in contributing to the country's economy, but also in the strategic benefits of channeling Caspian oil through pipelines to Black Sea ports. Subsequently, the oil would be loaded onto tankers and transported to global markets via the Black Sea and the Turkish Straits. The practical efficiency of this new system would ultimately alleviate additional maritime traffic burden in the straits and mitigate the associated risks of maritime accidents and environmental pollution.

This was complicated by the "Declaration Regarding the Deepening Strategic Cooperation" that Heydar Aliyev had signed with Turkish PM Suleyman Demirel during his official visit to Turkey in May 1997. The cooperation included a unity of interests and consensus about various matters between the two countries and gave the first signal that the taken risk could succeed. The declaration stated that both sides desired Azerbaijan oil to be transported through Turkey. When Heydar Aliyev spoke in the Turkish Grand National Assembly to deputies, he showed his resolve on the matter once again: "Yesterday, on the agreement signed by the Presidents of Turkey and Azerbaijan, we wrote that we wanted this giant oil pipeline to be made on Baku-Ceyhan route." He also remarked, "I can also talk in your accent. But I purposefully don't, so that you all shall learn ours," which was significant as it pointed out how far future relations between the two countries could reach.

Could this situation result in favor of Turkey, meaning that Turkish Straits were freed of that extra traffic load Caspian oil would bring and the risks it would create? It is not possible to assume this, because Caspian oil was not limited only to Azerbaijani oil. There was also the matter of Kazakhstani oil.

Kazakhstan adopted a versatile foreign policy strategy after the Soviets dissolved. Within this framework, they managed to form relations with global actors like the United States of America and the European Union. Besides, they kept their relations with their two big neighbors Russia and China warm. The architect of this strategy was Nursultan Nazarbayev, the last leader of Kazakhstan during the Soviet Union period and the country's first president after independence. In this period, Kazakhstan prioritized developing the potential of the Tengiz oil fields, which reside on the Caspian Sea's northeast banks, to recover their economy. The first step was taken in 1992 to this end. Kazakhstan faced similar challenges with Azerbaijan, as not having any shores on open seas near their oil fields. The Caspian Pipeline Consortium (CPC) was founded in conjunction with Russia and Oman for the construction of an oil transporting line from Tengiz region of Kazakhstan to Novorossiysk. The next and most important step was taken on April 6, 1993. Nazarbayev and Kenneth T. Derr, Chairman of American oil company Chevron, signed a deal to form a Kazakh American joint initiative towards improving Tengiz fields. This initiative, named Tengizchevroil (TCO), was formed as a half-and-half partnership between KazakhOil, the state oil company, and Chevron.

When the oil that belongs to their immediate surroundings is being shared and transported, it would naturally be unthinkable for Russia not to intervene in this case. Nazarbayev had friendly relations with Russia and some portion of Kazakhstan's population is of Russian origin. Accordingly, Russia used a different and more subtle strategy, similar to the one in Azerbaijan, instead of intervening in domestic politics. They would impede the oil pipeline through Russian soil to Black Sea from realization.

TCO overcame obstacles like the excessive depth, high pressure, and extreme level of sulfur concentration of Tengiz reservoir to begin producing and exporting. However, in the meantime, the CPC (which included Russia) failed – ironically – to get a Russian permit for the pipeline construction. Russia was already earning money from transportation since Tengiz oil was exported entirely through their own soil, mostly via railway. So, they had no need to rush. Under these circumstances, operations in Tengiz needed to be shuffled. CPC was reconstructed in 1996 with the accession of eight new companies. While American, European, and Russian companies had a combined 50% share, the other half was divided between Russia, Kazakhstan, and Oman. TCO expanded into a four-company initiative after the accession of ExxonMobil (USA), and LukArco – a joint initiative by Lukoil and Arco (USA). After these developments, there stood almost no obstacles for the construction of the Tengiz-Novorossiysk pipeline. Meanwhile, a supplementary deal was signed in May 1997 regarding the financing of the pipeline. But the road was being travelled, and the point it arrived at was pleasing for Kazakhstan and Russia, along with all the companies within CPC and TCO. The US was disturbed that Russia would achieve an important gain on the path to becoming a monopoly for the Western-transporting pipelines of Caspian oil. Moreover, the danger that high tanker traffic would transform the Turkish Straits into an oil pipeline was significantly worrying for Turkey.

It would of course be fanciful to expect the US to stand idly by. The multiple pipeline strategy offered and applied in Azerbaijan could also be applied in Kazakhstan. Already pursuing a versatile foreign policy and not considering dependance on a single country to maintain their oil export, Kazakhstan considered different options on its agenda as well. At this point, the question arose whether the two countries could find common ground. The answer to that was given soon enough, in October 1998, when the Ankara Declaration was signed, which included Caspian oil being transported to world markets via the Baku-Ceyhan pipeline. This declaration, witnessed by Bill Richardson, US Secretary of Energy, was signed by Turkey, Azerbaijan, Kazakhstan, Georgia, and Uzbekistan presidents (Suleyman Demirel, Heydar Aliyev, Nursultan Nazarbayev, Eduard Shevardnadze, and Islam Karimov, respectively). Although the construction of the Caspian Pipeline Consortium began in May 1999, Turkey covered quite a distance with the Ankara Declaration regarding Azerbaijan oil's transportation through Turkish territory and was on the verge of being chosen as an alternative for some of Kazakhstani oil to be transported on the same line.

After the declaration, another obstacle came before the materialization of the Baku-Ceyhan pipeline: British giant BP did not find the line economical. But this was not an insurmountable problem, and the US convinced them. This led to November 1999, at the Organization for Security and Co-operation summit in Europe (OSCE), where Demirel, Aliyev and Shevardnadze signed the framework agreement which foresaw how Azerbaijani oil would flow from Tbilisi to Ceyhan. US President Bill Clinton also witnessed to the deal.

The construction of the Tengiz-Novorossiysk pipeline was completed in March 2001, and oil pumping began. In November, the first tanker with Tengiz oil set out to sea from Novorossiysk harbor. Now Turkey had nothing to do but hope that the construction of the Baku-Tbilisi-Ceyhan (BTC) pipeline would begin as soon as possible and get done as quickly. This would take a long time. Indeed, the construction would only begin in September 2003, and the line would not become active until 2006.

Nevertheless, it is worth mentioning one point here, within this long and arduous process in which all the dreams Turkey had placed come true, and everything fell into place: There is an undeniable fact that while the US strategy of transporting both Azerbaijan and Kazakhstan oil via multiple pipelines, was done for the regional stability and the security of global energy supply (along with looking after their own interest), at the same time the US still protected Turkey, as their ally, and sided with them when Turkey strived to take Turkish Straits Regulations out of IMO agenda during the same process.

Varyag's time in Turkey coincided with the exact period when Turkey wanted to demonstrate their jurisdiction to inspect and judge without any contradiction of Montreux Convention regulations. This heightened concerns about the limitation of Turkey's sovereignty rights with only passage and transportation on the Straits. And one bureaucrat, having caught attention with his firm stance, deserves special mention.

Ruhan Cakiroglu was born in 1952 in the Of district in the Black Sea province of Trabzon. He was a maritime expert with a bachelor's degree in civil engineering. Cakiroglu served various duties in the public bureaucracy and acted as a unit expert in Deniz Nakliyat TAS's Department of Agencies before being appointed as Istanbul District Manager of the Turkish Maritime Undersecretariat, a critically important seat for Varyag. Deniz Nakliyat was founded in 1955 and acted as a school for developing Turkish maritime works. The company was privatized in 1993. After the Close Monitoring Agreement which Turkey signed with the IMF, it was chosen among the institutions to be privatized immediately, and then in 2000, was sold by tender procedure to Armatorler Denizcilik ve Nakliyat AS (Shipowners Maritime and Transportation, Inc.).

Having to leave Deniz Nakliyat after the privatization, Ruhan Cakiroglu was offered a very prestigious job: Directorate General of Coastal Safety. However, the proposal, which Cakiroglu had welcomed, would not become a reality. The 57th Government (AnaSol-M) was in power, with DSP, MHP and ANAP as coalition partners. The Directorate General of Coastal Security, headed by maritime lawyer Hucum Tulgar, was under the control of the MHP. Ruhan Cakiroglu actually had a worldview close to MHP. But some forceful people within the party frowned on his prospective position. In the end, Hucum Tulgar carried on his duty, and Cakiroglu was appointed as Istanbul District Manager on May 15, 2000. This date coincided with something interesting: one of the last decrees that the 9th President of Republic of Turkey, Suleyman Demirel, had approved before he completed his duty was Cakiroglu's commission of appointment, signed by PM Bulent Ecevit, Vice PM and MHP Leader Devlet Bahceli, and Minister Ramazan Mirzaoglu.

Getting appointed with a four-way decree – characteristic of coalition cabinets, in which coalition partners approve of appointments made by each other – Ruhan Cakiroglu found the sixteen-month-long matter of "Varyag's passage through Turkish Straits" dropped in his lap, so to speak. This passage was under Istanbul District Manager's jurisdiction, and the jurisdiction was run by the "Vessel Survey Board" under the management. Among the duties of the board was the determination of passage rules for ships that requested towing passage through Bosphorus. Cakiroglu called for an investigation within his organization for this giant carrier that had been towed to Turkish territorial waters and had a towing

THE GREAT GAME

passage request via agency shortly after his duty began. The first request from 1998 arrived. Thereupon Cakiroglu examined the case and studied the information about Varyag. As explained in previous chapters, this first request had seen a negative outcome for the Chong Lot company. Cakiroglu's examination also revealed the reason for the rejection of the solicitor agency's request: The General Staff had not approved the Varyag's passage.

Moreover, Cakiroglu did not settle with the information on the case file and made additional investigations through IMO and Chernomorsky Shipyard. According to him, Varyag was an "aircraft carrier" that had its engines and turbines but lacked weapon systems and other electric and electronic components. Its steering mechanism was disassembled intentionally so that it cannot go on its route by its own functions. It had been made to look like a simple hull, but in a way that did not qualify as a "vessel." However, it could still very well be turned into a fully functional aircraft carrier. In this respect, it would be negligent to define the ship as a simple hull or overlook, while ignoring its original functionality, or to not understand its possible intended purpose. According to the Montreux Convention, the vessel couldn't pass through Turkish Straits in its original state as an aircraft carrier. Hence China followed such a method.

For this reason, Ruhan Cakiroglu, as a qualified and idealistic bureaucrat, did not lean towards Varyag's passage at first. Cakiroglu thought, "No one can pass through these straits as they please," and stood against the attempts to ignore Turkey's sovereignty rights that the Montreux Convention had recognized.

Another issue that disturbed Cakiroglu was Caspian oil, previously explained in detail. Because he was aware of the burden and risks that Caspian oil, when transported on tankers, would bring to the straits.

Cakiroglu knew that dozens of tankers with 930 feet length and 230 feet width were being constructed around the world due to the expected volume of Caspian oil reserves. The production levels, therefore, would only increase in time. Cakiroglu was also informed about INTERTANKO's (The International Association of Independent Tanker Owners) opposition to the construction of the Baku-Tbilisi-Ceyhan pipeline. Besides, the struggle made in international platforms to establish Turkish Straits Regulations in practice has just been won. Indeed, when the matter was later discussed in Turkish media, various experts commented that "if Varyag's passage is permitted, it would pave the way for other vessels of the same size to get permission."

To transport Caspian oil via low-cost seaway, instead of pipelines, meant that the Turkish Straits would be bargained away to tanker accidents. In fact, on November 15, 1979, the tanker Independenta, carrying 95,000 tons of oil to Romania, had collided with Greek dry cargo vessel Evriali while the latter was coming from Black Sea. The former exploded with a massive noise. The accident had cost 43 crew members' lives. At the same time, the fire that carried on for almost a month, along with the crude oil spilt on the sea, was a serious environmental disaster.

Cakiroglu asked for an opinion from the Maritime Undersecretariat – the authority he reported to – before convening the Vessel Survey Board to discuss Varyag's towing passage. However, it did not go as he had expected as the Undersecretariat responded that Varyag should be allowed to pass. The Cakiroglu-led Board evaluated the case regarding passage safety through the straits and, despite the Undersecretariat's affirming stance, opted against Varyag's passage. The Chinese camp had no other solution than re-requesting for Varyag, still stuck in the Black Sea, to reach China. Indeed, right after this rejection, they made their second request and contracted with Aybay & Aybay Law Office to be able to pursue the matter in terms of the law. Gunduz Aybay, a maritime lawyer and a sea captain, was a member of the team that had worked effectively for Turkish Straits Regulation to be accepted by both domestic law and IMO. China had chosen the most suitable law office for this work.

Despite these moves by China, it was inevitable that Cakiroglu would stand by his decision since he had based it on the security and strategy risks of a potential passage.

With the second request, the Maritime Undersecretariat's opinion was asked again. They sent a quite detailed (from a to z, in Cakiroglu's words) study about how Varyag could be assisted through the straits securely. And that is what makes the piece interesting. The Undersecretariat had prepared the study that the Vessel Survey Board should normally have made – and without jurisdiction, at that. Moreover, only the Istanbul District Management had an authorized Vessel Survey Board.

At this moment, other developments were occurring behind the scenes. The Secretariat had asked the General Staff and Foreign Ministry for their opinions before sending that second study to District Management. The General Staff had responded negatively. They believed that Varyag's passage would not only be "unsafe or undesirable" but "impossible." At that time, the Ministry of Foreign Affairs, which was in favor of allowing the passage, expressed concern that the rejection would create problems between the two countries. The issue had now become a tangled web between state institutions. At a point where many bureaucrats would have hesitated to take initiative, Cakiroglu did not change his stance and clearly expressed his attitude with the words "This ship can only pass under the state's direct control and formal administration." and the giant ship was not allowed to pass again. After the second rejection, the matter was dispatched by the Undersecretariat to Minister of Maritime Affairs, Ramazan Mirzaoglu. The Varyag affair was already in the process of rapidly spreading into the Turkish and global agenda. Having briefly explained his stance on the matter before, Minister Mirzaoglu stated his approach to the press in these words:

"This vessel is a hull rather than a ship. Varyag does not have steering or engine and will be towed through. Until today, no ship longer than 1,000 feet was allowed to pass. So if we allow one, which amounts to an overall length of 1,800 feet including the towing and steering tugs, what would happen to Istanbul? The Bosphorus has very sharp turns and rips currents. That hull could not be managed. Twelve million lives are at stake here. Nature and history are at stake. We cannot disregard them. If the ship crashes somewhere, it cannot be salvaged for at least six months."

As a person who attached importance to merit, Mirzaoglu stood behind the bureaucracy's call. And, despite acting in favor of Varyag's passage from the beginning, the Maritime Undersecretariat would also act under the minister.

The now-former minister wrote about his support for Cakiroglu's decision on November 4, 2015, in his column on the online news portal medyagunlugu.com:

"Istanbul District Manager could have given the passage permits. But it was impossible for Varyag to pass through the Bosphorus safely. In that sense, the matter was brought to me as the minister of maritime affairs. We did not allow the passage."

The matter was now on the governmental agenda. Mirzaoglu narrates the atmosphere and developments in upper levels of government regarding Varyag's passage in the same column piece:

"The matter was brought to the government's attention. Minister Sukru Sina Gurel, I as a minister, and Deputy Chief of General Staff General Yasar Buyukanit assembled under the chairmanship of Late PM Bulent Ecevit to discuss the matter. Despite Foreign Affairs' positive opinion, both our Ministry and General Staff opposed it because this engineless, steerless, giant hull would be dangerous while passing, especially on Bosphorus. Therefore, the ship's passage was not permitted. According to the Montreux Convention, Turkish Straits' control, security, and sea traffic falls under Turkey's responsibility. The passage is unrestricted, but security is imperative.

"China was insistent on towing the carrier away. The Chinese Ambassador kept coming to the ministry and prime ministry, making many promises. But to no avail. I was invited to China several times regarding the matter. I did not accept those invitations. After that, they invited firstly the Commander of Naval Forces Full Admiral Ilhami Erdil, then Chief of General Staff Huseyin Kivrikoglu, and then one of the vice PMs. After these visits, our PM assembled us again – as the roster mentioned above. This time the General Staff representative changed his opinion. I stood alone. But still, I listed the precautions to be taken for a safe passage through Bosphorus."

In June 2001, Chief of General Staff Huseyin Kivrikoglu visited China. The trip, made after Chinese People's Liberation Army Chief of General Staff Fu Quanyou's invitation, was presented as "looking toward possibilities of military cooperation between the countries." During the five-day visit, Kivrikoglu also met with Chinese Head of State Jiang Zemin. In the meeting, Jiang said that Kivrikoglu's visit would definitely serve to develop the relations between the two countries and armies even further. At the same time, Kivrikoglu reflected those exchanges and cooperation between the two armies should be strengthened at every level to help further develop relations between states. After this visit, Kivrikoglu remained on duty for one more year and retired in August 2002.

The possible reason behind Chief of General Staff's change of heart was said to be one of China's promises: Turkey would get two million Chinese tourists per annum. The country, in an economic turndown, needed this. The ironic part is that this promise of China never materialized. The year after Varyag's passage through the straits, only 31.995 Chinese tourists came to Turkey! And the person at the center of this promise was no other than Ambassador Yao, who had been asked to do the best he could, and went from door to door, as Mirzaoglu mentioned. Yao was actually promising to make an effort to turn Turkey into a tourism destination for Chinese citizens in a world where the Varyag was allowed to pass but he had not mentioned a specific number of tourists. In July 2001, Yao's promise made headlines in almost all national newspapers, along with a specific number of tourists. When papers wrote articles, they laid it on thick about the parallels between Yao's promise and a Turkish diplomat's words – "At first step, if only one percent of the 180 million annual foreign tourists was to come, Turkish tourism would soar." The diplomat attended meetings at the House of Foreign Affairs during Foreign Minister Tang's visit to Turkey, without much knowledge of the Chinese language. Thus, he was the seed of the "two million Chinese tourists" legend. In short, the promise alleged to be given by the Chinese government and shown as the reason for General Staff's change of heart had not existed.

As the General Staff's attitude contradicted their previously known stance, the Maritime Undersecretariat sent an annotation to General Staff, asking them to state their opinions clearly. The response that reached the Undersecretariat the next day stated that they leaned towards Varyag's passage through the straits. But this could only happen "if risks are minimized and under certain conditions." General Staff's annotation mentioned that Varyag, lacking both engine and steering equipment, could pass through the straits by minimising risks that might threaten security of life, property, environment, and cruise. The conditions were set as such:

"The vessel must have a pilot, the visibility must be at least five sea miles, five tugs must accompany the vessel, both straits must be closed to traffic, and the vessel must carry neither any fuel nor inflammable or explosive substances."

Due to the changed conditions in the second meeting, PM Ecevit also gave a written directive to Mirzaoglu for the safe passage of Varyag. Even if he now stood alone, Mirzaoglu still said that his reservations persisted, and that a safe passage was impossible under existing conditions. However, on August 24, Ecevit sent a second note to notify him that Varyag's passage was permitted. Along with this, the PM's Office conveyed

THE GREAT GAME

Ecevit's decision to the Embassy of China by phone. The next day, Government Spokesperson and Minister Sukru Sina Gurel left for Australia with a delegation, having been invited there to determine the problems of Australian Turks and to find solutions. He had been scheduled to move on to China after his meetings in Australia and meet with Turkish businesspeople in Beijing, Shanghai, and Hong Kong. But at that point, a new agenda item was added: to convey Ecevit's "decision to permit Varyag's passage" to the Chinese government as official information. It is also known that during his China visit, Gurel also went to Macau and visited Macau World Trade Center.

After Ecevit's approval, China was swift to act. Without waiting for Sukru Sina Gurel's arrival, the government sent Hong Shanaxiang, Vice Transportation Minister, and Maritime Minister, to Turkey. The first person that Hong would met was Mirzaoglu. Upon Hong's request, the meeting took place on August 28, and lasted twenty minutes. In that time, Mirzaoglu stressed, "this passage is permitted by PM Bulent Ecevit's directions and consent upon People's Republic of China's insistent demands." He further informed that in the case that both the technical conditions required for Varyag's passage were met and that weather and sea conditions were also suitable, then Varyag's passage could be made. Mirzaoglu added that delegations from the two countries would meet to work out the technical conditions, and the Turkish delegation would decide whether they could meet. For his part, Minister Hong thanked the Turkish government for placing importance on the relations between the two countries and making this accommodation before giving a vague response to a question made about two million Chinese tourists by saying they were in contact with the Foreign Ministry. After getting a positive reply at his meeting with Mirzaoglu, Hong would get a new duty in the upcoming days: Leading the Chinese delegation.

The process would now carry on with meetings between Turkish and Chinese technical delegations. In September, a commission led by Ruhan Cakiroglu was formed with experts from Istanbul District Management and other relevant agencies. On September 11, a mixed delegation featuring Ruhan Cakiroglu, Coastal Safety's Head of Salvage Department Arslan Dede, a sea captain, two senior pilots and an expert from Turkish Maritime Organisation, an official from Chong Lot, an insurance company executive, and two experts made investigations on Varyag. During those very hours, the US was shocked by the September 11 Attacks. Terrorists had hijacked American passenger planes and crashed into World Trade Center's twin towers in New York, killing thousands. Comments made after the passage argued that "Varyag could not have passed if it was not for these attacks"; these comments ultimately have no basis in truth, since the attack happened after Varyag had already been greenlit.

After technical investigations were made, commission members prepared a report containing twenty items of necessity for Varyag's safe passage through straits. Among them were: tugs to be assigned in previously required numbers, vessel hull to be lit, a capstan mechanism to be installed for line-throwing and hauling it back in, to have a generator present for lighting and capstan mechanism, a telecommunication network to be established onboard along with certain environmental conditions, such as no fog during passage, wind velocity to be suitable for known criteria, and visibility range no less than five sea miles.

The Turkish technical delegation conveyed the 20-item list of commission demands to the Chinese delegation led by Hong Shanaxiang. The Chinese delegation accepted all the obligatory demands, as they had no other choice. They were disturbed by the first item on the list. The Maritime Undersecretariat asked China for a one-billion-dollar security deposit that would be valid for two years for any possible damages during Varyag's passage. The Chinese delegation made a counteroffer to change the deposit with a state guarantee. The Foreign Ministry was aware of the situation and saw the state guarantee as suitable. At this point the Undersecretariat and Ministry were at cross purposes, Sukru Sina Gurel, tasked with following the affair by Ecevit, intervened and solved the issue. A state guarantee would be taken from China. Another clause was added: in case of an accident, the damage would be determined by Turkish courts. And details about the manner of financial collection were also determined.

The meeting between the Turkish and Chinese delegations took place on September 26. The Chinese delegation stated there that they would grant, instead of a state guarantee, a Chong Lot company guarantee. They informed relevant Turkish posts about the matter – indicating the Foreign Ministry. Later in the meeting, the report that was written by commission members who inspected Varyag was examined to check whether the technical demands for safe passage were met. None of these demands were "seriously" addressed. As a consequence, the Turkish delegation openly expressed to the Chinese delegation that Turkey's demands, including the state guarantee, were not matters of negotiation.

Meanwhile, the matter was being discussed in the Council of Ministers. In other words, as Ruhan Cakiroglu – who kept up the classic resolve of Black Sea people until the end – wished, "at the government's disposal." With PM Bulent Ecevit's instructions, a Council of Ministers Principle Resolution was prepared and opened for signatures. According to constitutional precedents (among sources of Turkish Constitutional Law), Council of Ministers Principle Resolutions were prepared about matters discussed in the Council of Ministers. But they are not required to be turned into a decree to be submitted for the president's approval. There were often non-executory, explanatory resolutions for relevant public institutions and organisations. Thus, these sorts of decrees are not required to be published in the official gazette. But Mirzaoglu persistently refused to sign said resolution for Varyag's passage, which had been roaming around Black Sea steerless and engineless for the last sixteen months. So, how could the carrier pass through the straits? Let us quote in Mirzaoglu's words:

"Meanwhile, I was on a visit to a foreign country. Unfortunately, they made the fellow minister who deputized me sign the Council of Ministers Resolution regarding Varyag's passage. Varyag was passed through the straits with multiple tugs. By chance, no accidents happened."

The person who "deputized" Ramazan Mirzaoglu was Husnu Yusuf Gokalp from MHP, then Minister of Agriculture and Rural Affairs. On October 1, Mirzaoglu had left for Sudan to attend the opening of the Turkish Exported Goods Fair. Another minister, one from his own party at that, had put the very signature Mirzaoglu resisted against. At this time, the Varyag's passage had no obstacles other than the Chinese side themselves.

Council of Ministers Principle Resolution numbered P.2001/6, signed by PM Bulent Ecevit and thirty-five ministers, four of them deputized, was as follows:

"It has been resolved by the Council of Ministers on October 5, 2001 that safe passage of the floating object with unfinished construction named Varyag, previously sold by Ukraine to a company resident in People's Republic of China, will be ensured with the precautions determined by the delegation of technical experts formed by Prime Ministry Undersecretariat of Maritime Affairs, and the accident risk reduced as much as possible The State Guarantee of People's Republic of China will be received by Ministry of Foreign Affairs for damages our country might have The matter will be pursued within relevant ministry's responsibility."

After the Council of Ministers granted the passage permit, the Chinese camp reported that technical conditions are completed. Thereupon, members of the commission led by Ruhan Cakiroglu, along with the Chinese delegation, got on Varyag, which was towed outside Turkish territorial waters by Solano that had assumed Sandy Cape's duty on September 14th. It was seen that some of the conditions were not met yet, but China, knowing the passage would get harder as the winter approached, was anxious to eliminate the deficiencies. Besides,

Varyag's date of passage would be determined after the commission's positive report for approval.

Among all these developments, something that almost never came to the fore was the condition of the Sandy Cape crew, who had been stuck in the Black Sea for over a year, towing Varyag. The crew was comparing Varyag to the Alcatraz, the famous prison commonly depicted in motion pictures as being impossible to escape. For them, Varyag was little more than that, even in spite of the fact that ITC, the towing contractor, tried to carry out regular crew changes out of Istanbul, which in a way was illegal to do outside the territorial waters of Turkey...

Stuck in the Black Sea, the crew witnessed also some interesting incidents. The most significant of those was an unidentified, mysterious helicopter that landed on Varyag in early July. Some people had come down from it and carried out some measurements before getting off the carrier, but they also left a note written with chalk: "The French were here." It still remains a mystery who wrote it. But the helicopter might be tracked back to figure out from which Black Sea country it had taken off.

A photograph in ITC director Joop Timmermans' private album gives some access to information about the helicopter. The photo was taken a short while before the helicopter's unauthorized landing on Varyag's deck. Although it was impossible to read its tail number, indication of Bell 206B JetRanger still could be detected. The same model of helicopter was spotted on November 1, 2001, as the aircraft in Varyag's closest pursuit while Varyag was passing through Bosphorus. However, only the helicopters that were on duty that day were allowed to fly above Varyag if necessary. It was forbidden for other aircraft to fly near the vessel or make recordings. Now it has become obvious that the helicopter must have taken off from Istanbul. The agency which had pursued Varyag's passage through the straits was given special permission so that Chinese officials could observe the process in the air. The

VARYAG

helicopter was rented from the hotel the officials stayed at. This hotel that owned the helicopter was considered the Istanbul branch of a world-famous chain. Their helicopter was obtained from an aviation company and used to transport their customers to and from the airports and to make tours within Istanbul. It is very likely that the people who left the mysterious message would have stayed in this hotel.

Mysterious landing on Varyag's flight deck. *Photo from the album of Joop Timmermans.*

CHAPTER 7

PASSAGE

The Bosphorus has witnessed a large number of marine accidents, as it is navigationally one of the roughest and most dangerous waterways. Due to differences of sea level and salinity between the Marmara and the Black Sea, this strait's undercurrents have undertows, flowing in the opposite direction of surface currents. There are also reverse crosscurrents due to the Bosphorus' indented structure, and riffles impacted by occasional strong southern winds – primarily southwestern. Under these circumstances, the variable factors of Bosphorus, such as wind, current, and range of vision, limit the manoeuvrability of passing vessels and increase accident risk. Varyag's voyage through the straits, accompanied by tugs, was already set to be very difficult. To prevent these challenging conditions from further hampering Varyag's passage, very strict and clear criteria were set: Wind velocity had to be below five knots, current velocity had to be below three knots, and range of vision had to be above five nautical miles. If these criteria were met, the countdown would start. However, what exactly happened to get to this point?

After the inspections and findings of the Turkish commission members on Varyag, the Chinese side belatedly recognized that they ought to meet with the technical demands that Turkey requested in writing. They managed to complete the specified missing parts in the third week of October. After the review of reports and planning for Varyag's passage, two rehearsals were conducted on October 22 and 29 with the whole crew and equipment present to minimize possible risks on the straits. Then it was only a matter of waiting for adequate weather and sea conditions for Varyag to be towed through the Turkish Straits.

In the evening hours of October 31, officers of the undersecretariat, experts, Turkish Maritime Organisation (TDI) General Directorate officers, and head maritime pilots all gathered in the Turkish Undersecretariat of Maritime Affairs' Istanbul District Office. This meeting was held to evaluate the available data and estimates. It was decided that weather conditions and the current velocity on and around the Bosphorus would be adequate on November 1, 2001, and Varyag would be towed behind tugboats within agreed parameters at the first light of day. With the decision, this impetuous passage would be conducted under Istanbul District Office's coordination and under the guidance, organization and management of the maritime pilots from TDI Istanbul Port Management, who had attended rehearsals in October.

Ensuring thousands of vessels' safe passage through Turkish Straits each year thanks to their local knowledge and experience, maritime pilots would, this time, work as a team to transit Varyag with tugboats. Leading the operating team was Head Maritime Pilot Saim Oguzulgen, the director of the trials before passage who had captained domestic and foreign-flagged vessels before beginning to serve as a maritime pilot for Istanbul Port Management in 1982 and who had also been acting as TDI Vice-General Manager for three years. Devoting himself to his profession and Turkish Straits, Oguzulgen had served within the workgroup formed to prepare Regulations for the Turkish Straits in 1990, and acted as a technical expert in the delegation that oversaw Turkish Straits Maritime Traffic Separation Scheme meetings at IMO between 1993 and 1999.

On November 1, 2001, at 04:00, preparations to go to Varyag's location in the Black Sea began under Head Maritime Pilot Oguzulgen's lead. At 04:30, head maritime pilots, including Oguzulgen, other maritime pilots, and Istanbul

PASSAGE

District Office authorities boarded tugs named Poyraz and Kiz Kulesi at Port of Karakoy, from the part of the Bosphorus closest to Marmara and headed towards Varyag. Minutes passed, as the convoy formed with other tugs under maritime pilots from different points of departure. At 06:20, around Buyukdere near Bosphorus' Black Sea exit, the tugs named Gemi Kurtaran, Kurtarma 1, Kurtarma 2, and Sonduren 4 of Coastal Safety and Vessel Salvage Management joined the convoy and voyaged towards Varyag. At 06:45, just after sunup, they passed the Turkeli (or Rumeli) Lighthouse at the northernmost point of Bosphorus. In the meantime, at 05:00, Varyag began being towed by the tug Havila Champion and was escorted by the tugs Nikolay Chiker and Solano. Varyag had moved only four nautical miles down Bosphorus after having set sail from the international waters of the Black Sea. Havila Champion and Nikolay Chiker tugs had been taken into service by China to address the requirement regarding the adequate number of tugs, in the conditions Turkey set. At 07:30, about 2.5 nautical miles off Turkeli Lighthouse, the two convoys met.

The officers and maritime pilots who would serve on Varyag and accompanying tugs took their duty positions. A meeting was held on Varyag's flybridge. This was the deck above the navigating bridge where the ship's management took place, and it had been chosen as the operation headquarters. In this meeting, after reviewing the most recent data from the General Directorate of State Meteorology Affairs, it was decided that weather conditions and current velocity at hand (southern and south-eastern winds of 4 knot, current velocity of 1.2-1.3 knot, and range of vision above 5 nautical miles) were suitable for passage. The official intention, written and signed by attendees, resolved that the operation to pass Varyag through the 17-nautical-miles-long Bosphorus, first of the Turkish Straits, would be initiated at 09:00.

First instructions of the operation were given to Havila Champion, which would act as the leading tugboat in charge of towing Varyag through Turkish Straits, and Nikolay Chiker, which would serve as the rudder and stopper at the stern, to shorten their towing ropes, and the tugs serving at Varyag's bow and quarter were told to belay their ropes to the carrier.

Around 08:45, Havila Champion, Kurtarma 1, and Kurtarma 2 tugs at the bow, and Nikolay Chiker, Poyraz, and Kiz Kulesi on the stern side were ready for duty; and also, backup tugs, fire extinguishing tugs, and boats of Coastal Safety and Coast Guard which would serve for security had all taken position. After a small-scale rehearsal, the voyage toward the entrance of the Bosphorus slowly began with the signal by Oguzulgen. A short while later, when it was seen that the system consisting of Varyag and her six tugs was sailing smoothly, the tugboat Havila Champion was told to increase speed.

While these developments occurred in the convoy, the Bosphorus was closed from both ways to the passage of non-stopover vessels at 08:00 as previously planned, and City Lines ferries were temporarily suspended. Istanbulites wishing to watch Varyag's passage had rushed to coastlines on both sides of the city from the early hours on and were waiting for the convoy with curiosity and anticipation.

The big moment had arrived. When the clock struck 10:10, the convoy passed by the line of lighthouses – between Turkeli and Anatolia Lighthouses – at the northern entrance of the strait and entered Bosphorus. The entrance began with a very light south-wester wind, and everyone was glad that weather and sea conditions were even better than expected. The convoy progressed under Saim Oguzulgen's management. As a maritime professional, Oguzulgen could share the emotion that the other captains felt as they maneuvered their ships. At the same time, boats and vessels of the maritime police, coast guard, and port authority cautioned fishing boats and other vessels away from the convoy's route. Ruhan Cakiroglu, who facilitated this complex and formidable coordination, was following the operation from a boat of Coast Guard and Vessel Salvage Management.

As the passage began, many journalists, domestic and foreign, were reporting. They followed it step by step and filmed it all along the Bosphorus for media outlets. National networks such as CNN Turk and NTV were live broadcasting the passage from both the shore and the air by helicopter with running technical commentary from experts. However, this historic passage was not documented only by those. Ikonos, an earth observation satellite operating 423 miles above, had been tasked with filming Varyag while she was towed through the strait.

Satellite imagery of Varyag crossing the Bosphorus. *Image by INTA Space Systems.*

VARYAG

Designed and built by Lockheed Martin Commercial Space Systems, one of the largest defense industry corporations in the world for Space Imaging, Inc. and sent to space in 1999, Ikonos was the first ever public-access sub-meter high-resolution earth observation satellite. Varyag's filming was conducted by the earth station of Space Imaging Eurasia, also known as INTA Space Systems, which had only recently been put into service in Golbasi, Ankara. INTA was founded by Cukurova Holding and Uydusan partnership to deal with Ikonos' regional management and sale of its images. One day after the passage, on November 2, Varyag's photos in all shapes and sizes, captured from Earth's orbit, was not only giving a taste of the passage to readers with Bosphorus' peerless beauty but also indicating the capabilities of a private satellite in competition with military spy satellites.

Progressing at the speed of 3.5 knots, the system reached the Beykoz-Umuryeri turn at 11:40. This has previously been considered one of the riskier points of the passage. Here Varyag's turn was managed ponderously, but without any problem. The southwester wind had accelerated slowly around noon, though not enough to affect the convoy's voyage.

Not long after the successful completion of the first risky turn, this time, the convoy reached the cape of Yenikoy-Koybasi, also known as the turn of Yenikoy. This happens to be Bosphorus' most critical point for southbound – from the Black Sea to the Marmara – non-stopper vessels, where they are obliged to change course with an eighty-degree angle. But it wasn't the sharpness of the turn that was the major issue here. Instead, it was the high possibility that Varyag's bow and stern could succumb to different currents during the turn. Slowing before the turn, Varyag's change of route, with a wide angle and as gently as possible, was completed at 12:33.

At 12:51, Istinye, a coastal district on the European side, was passed, and the convoy reached the narrowest part of the Bosphorus, which began from Kanlica district on the Anatolian side and stretched on with a 0.6-nautical-mile width for approximately 4.3 nautical miles until reaching the Bosphorus Bridge.

At 13:12, Varyag passed 36 feet under the mid-section – 210-feet-high from sea level – of Fatih Sultan Mehmet Bridge, the 554-feet-high suspended bridge that is the second connection between Asia and Europe after the Bosphorus Bridge.

At 13:20, the convoy, at the speed of 2.5 knots, entered between Anatolian Fortress and Rumeli Fortress, the narrowest place on Bosphorus at 2,293 feet with a high current velocity. According to experts, this was the riskiest part of the operation. When the system first passed by the Cape of Kandilli and then the Cape of Akinti at 13:35 without any problems, there was a collective sigh of relief.

Varyag, being towed (southbound) through the Bosphorus with the assistance of tugs. *Photo by Kerim Okten/EPA Images.*

At 14:00, Varyag was towed behind the midsection – that has the same height from sea-level as Fatih Sultan Mehmet Bridge – of 541-feet-high the Bosphorus Bridge, had been the fourth longest suspension bridge when it was put into service in 1973.

The southwestern wind had begun to die down, current velocity was slow, so Varyag's risk of drifting while turning had decreased considerably. Leaving the narrowest part of Bosphorus behind to carry on towards the Marmara Sea, the system passed by the Maiden's Tower at 14:30 and Ahirkapi Lighthouse, the oldest of Istanbul, at 14:45 with ease.

As the clock showed 15:15, the convoy reached the Marmara Sea, and hereby, the operation to tow Varyag through Bosphorus was successfully completed. An unprecedented thing happened with this operation that took five hours at 3.5 knots. In the history of Turkish Straits maritime pilotage, this was the first time 19 maritime pilots served simultaneously for a passage. During Varyag's pass through the Bosphorus, there were a total of eleven tugs – six tugs actively maneuvering with towing hawsers, two big tugs following these, two fire extinguishing tugs, and one open sea salvage tug – along with three coastguard boats and one mooring boat.

At 15:30, the tugs at Varyag's bow and quarters were told to disconnect the towing hawsers and sail close to Varyag, as they would not participate in the Marmara Sea passage. According to the plan, Havila Champion would continue towing at Varyag's bow as the main tug, and only Nikolay Chiker would keep its tow wire connected to carrier's stern in case of emergencies. Also, five maritime pilots who served during the Bosphorus passage returned to their original posts at pilotage stations, while Istanbul District Office authorities left Varyag to return at Dardanelles passage. After four maritime pilots on Varyag's flying bridge passed on to Havila Champion and Nikolay Chiker, at 15:45, the second stage of Varyag's towing through the Turkish Straits began: The 110 nautical-mile-long Marmara Sea passage.

The meteorology forecasts indicated that on November 2, 2001, the weather would take a turn for the worse, the northern wind would strengthen, and heavy downfall was expected. This meant the group had to accelerate for Varyag to pass Marmara safely. Even though Havila Champion sped up, the existing

PASSAGE

towing method limited the convoy's speed to a maximum of 4.8 knots. It was now necessary to change the original planning for the system's voyage through Marmara. This concern was conveyed to TDI General Management, Istanbul Port Management, and Istanbul District Office authorities. After some discussions there, it was decided that Nikolay Chiker would leave its towing wire and Varyag would continue to be towed behind Havila Champion. However, this was not enough. Towed by just one tug, the system's speed could only approach 5.4 knots.

At 18:00, the situation was negotiated among authorities once again, and a new plan was made. Tug Solano was bound from its bow to a hawsehole at Varyag's stern under required safety precautions. At 18:15, Solano began to push Varyag. Fifteen minutes later, the system's speed reached 5.8 knots, and it was observed that Varyag remained in Havila Champion's route. After navigating at this speed for a while, Solano was asked to accelerate more, and the system's speed reached 6 knots; however, this time, the carrier's bow was seen to diverge from the leading tugboat's route. Since cruising this way would be undesirable, the previous speed was set once more. With the evaluation at 19:15, the conclusion was that keeping the speed on 5.8 knots, they could pass the Marmara Sea smoothly, and carry on with the voyage.

In the morning hours of November 2, as the wind grew stronger, it became harder for Varyag to stay the course. After Istanbul District Office authorities including Ruhan Cakiroglu returned to Varyag at 08:45 via helicopter, maritime pilots who remained on Havila Champion and Nikolay Chiker also returned to the aircraft carrier. 4.5 nautical miles from the Gelibolu Lighthouse, which guides vessels entering Dardanelles, a similar meeting to the one before passing the Bosphorus took place on Varyag's flying bridge. Weather conditions and current velocity (northeaster wind of 4-5 knots, current velocity of 1.5 knots, and range of vision above 5 nautical miles) were suitable for passage. At 09:40, the group was slowly decelerated according to the decision. At 10:00, TDI's General Manager Erkan Arikan and maritime pilots of Dardanelles, who would replace their counterparts from Istanbul who had left Varyag, arrived at the floating platform to join the mission. With the newly completed crew, firstly, Solano was disconnected from Varyag, and all other tugs who had active duties during Bosphorus passage along with Nikolay Chiker were connected again with towing wires. The system's structure was kept, except for one factor: Nikolay Chiker, which was connected with a towing wire from its stern to Varyag's stern, had the Emre Omur tug bound to it from the bow to serve as a rudder. They could now begin the passage of Dardanelles, and the 37 nautical miles of Turkish Straits as the third and final stage.

Officers and head maritime pilots posing on the flybridge of Varyag before entering the Dardanalles Strait. *Photo from the album of Saim Oguzulgen.*

Having passed the Marmara Sea at an average speed of 5.3 knots, the convoy entered the Dardanelles at 5 knots at 10:55. After passing by Gelibolu Lighthouse at 11:05, the Galata and Karakova Lighthouses were also soon left behind. However, the Emre Omur tug, which was bound to Nikolay Chiker's bow to prevent it from drifting, was not performing with the desired efficiency, and therefore it was decided that its connecting rope would be disconnected. At 13:10, the system's speed was decelerated to 4.5 knots to make the navigation safer between Nara and Cape of Kilitbahir, the most critical part of Dardanelles. At 14:05, after passing the Akbas Lighthouse, the strengthening southern wind's speed reached up to 6 knots as the voyage continued towards the Cape of Nara. 'When it was 14:30, they turned at the Cape of Nara close to the shoal buoy at very low velocity, and every available means were used for Varyag to cruise on track through Kilitbahir and Cimenlik Castles, the narrowest part of Dardanelles at 0.7 nautical miles. At 15:05, the turn at Cape of Kilitbahir began. Even though this turn had been intended to be made at a closer distance to Kilitbahir, the group had drifted towards the opposite shore. However, no problems occurred, and at 15:30, the Cape of Kilitbahir was successfully turned. The heavy downpour began at 15:45. Seeing that the weather would get even worse, Oguzulgen took initiative and decided that the passage would be accelerated. Havila Champion picked up speed while bow and quarter tugs were steered adequately to serve the system's speed. Thus, with the further help of wind and current, this' speed reached 7.5 knots, and the navigation carried on without issue. When the Cape of Karanfil was passed at 15:55, Istanbul District Office authorities left Varyag on a helicopter. At 16:50, while passing Canakkale Martyrs' Memorial built in memory of Turkish soldiers killed in Battle of Gallipoli during WWI in 1915, all the staff, tugs, and vessels saluted the monument. The convoy was now approaching the Aegean Sea exit of Dardanelles. The operation was almost done, and ships were leaving the convoy. As the Martyrs' Memorial was passed, the fire extinguishing tugs left. Then, after Mehmetcik Lighthouse was passed, tugs and other vessels which were not connected to Varyag left the convoy. At 17:30, the system reached the Aegean Sea, and all tugs but Havila Champion disconnected their towing hawsers. Dardanelles passage was managed smoothly at an average speed of 5.1 knots, and here ended the maritime pilots' duty on Varyag. At 17:45, maritime pilots handed the baton to captains of Havila Champion and Solano. The departing captains would head off to Mehmetcik Pilotage Station with the Poyraz tug.

John Gray is shown here in the process of signing and delivering the formal document, under which he took total control of Varyag. After receiving the document, Saim Oguzulgen left Varyag for Havila Champion on a pilotage boat. This document marked the moment that the long operation was officially over for Turkey. Meanwhile, Captain John Gray did not neglect to congratulate Head Maritime Pilot Saim Oguzulgen for the successful completion of Varyag's towage, also handing him a letter in which he thanked him and all maritime pilots who participated in the operation. At 17:45, after the valediction, Oguzulgen and all of the maritime pilots gathered on the Poyraz tug to ship out towards Mehmetcik Pilotage Station, at the exit of the Dardanelles.

All head maritime pilots and maritime pilots resting at Mehmetcik Pilotage Station after the operation. *Photo from the album of Saim Oguzulgen.*

PASSAGE

Beginning at 09:00 on November 1, 2001, Varyag's towed passage through the Turkish Straits was completed in exactly 32.5 hours. The operational costs for the Chinese side were quite hefty. Before the operation, for tugs and other vessels involved in Varyag's passage, China paid a total of 1,440,000 USD – 800,000 to the Turkish Maritime Organisation and 640,000 to Coastal Safety and Vessel Salvage Management. In 2000, CSVSM had ranked 19th in Istanbul Corporate Tax rankings, but in 2001, with 21.1 trillion liras (14.5 million USD – then) of tax assessment, they ranked 9th among top ten taxpayers. Since TDI provided all their services in exchange for USD payments, this was due to revenue growth from devaluation in 2001, when the Turkish lira lost value in the face of USD, but the income from Varyag's passage also made a small contribution against this.

Although he had frowned on Varyag's passage from the beginning, Minister Mirzaoglu did not begrudge this smooth execution of an historically challenging passage. Instead, he offered his appreciation by sending this message to the people and institutions that participated in the passage:

"Regarding the passage of the platform named Varyag that People's Republic of China has purchased from Ukraine, through Turkish Straits, I would like to extend my appreciation and wish a continued success to Prime Ministry Maritime Undersecretary, Mustafa Korcak, PhD.; Deputy Undersecretary, Alparslan Kaya; General Manager, Taner Ciftci; Vice-General Manager, Fikret Hakguden; Istanbul District Manager, Ruhan Cakiroglu; Coast Guard Commander, Rear Admiral Yalcin Ertuna; General Manager for Coastal Safety and Vessel Salvage Management, Hucum Tulgar; Department Head, Arslan Dede; Turkish Maritime Organisation General Manager Erkan Arikan and Head Maritime Pilot, Saim Oguzulgen on account of maritime pilots who were in charge of the passage, for showing outstanding efforts in determining necessary precautions, including conditions of secure passage and guarantees for possible dangers, and ensuring the carrier's safe passage, without any accidents."

At this point, a huge weight was taken off Turkey's shoulders, whereas China had passed the most critical point in their actions toward owning Varyag.

CHAPTER 8

AIRCRAFT CARRIER STYLE

Having successfully passed through the Turkish Straits, Varyag would meet with bad surprises in the Aegean Sea between Turkey and Greece. On November 2, 2001, Friday at 17:45, Varyag was left to Havilla Champion, the tug which had led the convoy and served as the main tugboat in charge of towing. Its assigned position had been limited to the Turkish Straits only. The tug Solano was originally assigned to pull Varyag on the open seas. However, the Solano failed to connect to Varyag due to extreme maritime weather conditions. Instead, Havilla Champion carried on towing the giant platform.

That evening, they were holding off on the southern shores of Gokceada, the Turkish island on the north-east corner of the Aegean Sea, when they received news of imminent strong north-east winds. Next day, towards midnight, a strong storm with wind speeds reaching up to 50 knots caused the tow wire to break between Varyag and Havilla Champion. Unleashed like a floating mine, Varyag was taken over by giant waves up to 25 feet, drifting away out of control. She was nearing Skyros Island in Greece, and it was only a matter of time for her to ground or hit rocks. The Varyag at that point had seven crew members on board, three Russian, three Ukrainian, and one Filipino. With the gravity of the matter heightened, a helicopter of the Greek coastguard safely evacuated four of Varyag's seven crew members. Fortunately, Havilla Champion managed to reconnect to the floating mass on Sunday morning with ropes thrown from Varyag's deck. The Sandy Cape was deployed off

Crete Island and was also put to sea to join Varyag's convoy. On Tuesday, when weather and naval conditions recovered significantly, and discussions of Solano assuming the duty of tug were brought up once more. However, a serious accident occurred during this operation and devastatingly, it claimed the life of Aries Lima, a Portuguese mariner of Havilla Champion tug.

Despite the fact that Solano assumed the duty after the operation, when Sandy Cape joined the convoy and connected to Varyag, new plans were made. Solano would pass the baton to Nikolay Chiker, a tug managed by Russian Tsavliris. Rehired by China, Nikolay Chiker joined the convoy on November 8, and Solano was set free. Now, Varyag could continue her voyage behind Nikolay Chiker and Sandy Cape, through the Strait of Gibraltar connecting the Mediterranean and Atlantic, around the Cape of Good Hope at Africa's southernmost tip, towards the Strait of Malacca. This longer route was chosen instead of passage through the Suez Canal, the great artificial watercourse connecting the Mediterranean with the Red Sea that granted shorter and less dramatic access to the Indian Ocean. Why was this long and risky route chosen?

At this point, Egypt entered to play its part in the story. The reason behind Varyag's long voyage by the Cape of Good Hope was Egypt's attitude to the project. China had planned before to go through the Suez Canal, the shorter route. However, the Egyptian government would not have permitted an engineless, rudderless platform like Varyag, to go through there. No ships were allowed to be towed through Suez Canal, one of the busiest trade routes between Europe and Asia. The uniform rejection of China's insistent requests for an exception meant that Varyag had to go around the Cape of Good Hope. An accident in 2021 showed the accuracy of Egypt's said decision. Due to a sandstorm and adverse weather conditions, and with the range of vision decreased, the 1,312 feet container ship Ever Given of the international transportation corporation Evergreen crashed into the banks of the Suez Canal, causing the

AIRCRAFT CARRIER STYLE

channel to completely shut down marine traffic for six days. The estimates show that this grounding harmed global trade by around ten billion USD per day.

Even though the fierce storm on the Aegean Sea and not getting the clearance for Suez Canal proved the final rings of the string of bad luck, they also set the alarm bells ringing for the Chinese side. On November 24, 2001, 285-feet oceanic salvage tug Suijiu 201 left the Port of Guangzhou, the capital of southern Chinese Guangdong province, with its two captains and headed for South Africa's Port of Cape Town to join the convoy. Towards the end of that December, this tugboat waited for a few days off the Port of Cape Town, and when they heard that convoy was getting close, it set sail once more and, coming around the Cape of Good Hope, managed to connect with Varyag on December 27 despite challenging weather.

Now escorted by three tugs, Varyag began the final stage of her voyage. The convoy was about to reach their destination, but there was this one difference: instead of the original destination of Macau, they were now instructed to head for a port city with shipyards in Liaoning province... Dalian!

Considering the technical hardships of ship towing over long distances, adjusting the route to Dalian was even more challenging, since there was now the Strait of Taiwan to handle at the end of it. Passing through this strait would shorten the voyage considerably, but the atmosphere there was tense at the time – as it often is. Deciding to avoid all factors they could not control, and also conferring with their counterparts from Nikolay Chiker and Sandy Cape, the captains of Suijiu 201 headed to the East China Sea.

In February 2002, the convoy was caught in another storm while cruising on the Philippine Sea. On February 18, they sailed towards Taiwan's eastern waters against north-easter winds of gale force 7 to 8 and gigantic waves. Despite the convoy's slowdown, they navigated the East China Sea without incident.

Meanwhile, this journey of Varyag after South Africa was not done alone. Going past South Africa, Taiwan, and Japan, the convoy was often watched and accompanied by local planes, helicopters, and speedboats. Captains generally tended to ignore these, so long as the towage was not disrupted.

On February 27, they met with dense fog while entering the outer anchorage of Port of Dalian. Varyag had her last waiting period on this anchorage. Suijiu 201 constantly broadcast radio warnings to nearby ships, asking them to steer clear of them, which attracted many curious onlookers.

Among these spectators was Xu Zengping, Varyag's de jure owner. In the early hours of March 2, a crew of twenty including Xu and customs staff reached the convoy on its outer anchorage. After inspections and meetings, Nikolay Chiker and Sandy Cape transferred their duties to Port of Dalian's tugs and left Varyag.

At 05:00 on Sunday, March 3 Varyag was escorted by six tugs and a pilot boat and shifted from outer port and headed for the inner port. After several maneuvers, she was safely berthed to pier number 4 on the western part of Dalian's inner port.

On a different note, the lengthy and challenging journey of the Varyag, which commenced in June 2000 at Ukraine's Chernomorsky Shipyard and lasted 627 days, concluded satisfactorily for the Chinese side.

Varyag was delivered to China. Those who had followed the process up until this point expected the work on Varyag to begin immediately, but things did not turn out that way. Chinese Head of State Jiang Zemin had not approved of this purchase at first, and upon learning about the operation, and it was initiated behind his back with the attitude, "If we don't buy her, Taiwan will." Though he unwillingly approved it in the end, he did not forget what happened. This attitude of Zemin started Varyag's three-year wait in Dalian. Varyag was kept there without any work done on her for three years. And Zemin's attitude showed little to no softening over time, but his term was approaching an end.

AIRCRAFT CARRIER STYLE

Zemin served several duties due to the complicated government structure in China. He left the post of General Secretary of the Chinese Communist Party on November 15, 2002, the post of Head of State on March 15, 2003, and Chinese Communist Party Chairman of the Central Military Commission on September 19, 2004. All the while, Varyag waited for her fate behind the high wire-fences of pier number 4. She was still catching the attention of many curious eyes. While the giant ship was waiting on pier number 4, many pictures taken from high buildings surrounding the port were shared online. It was interesting that China, infamously sensitive to their privacy, was not intervening in these actions.

At the 16th Central Committee of the Communist Party of China, held in 2002, Hu Jintao was appointed as General Secretary of the CCP, succeeding Zemin. Just as Zemin, he was a candidate for the supreme leadership of China, assuming the duties of Head of State and Chairman of the Central Military Commission consecutively, which brought Varyag back to the agenda. Appointed as vice president in 1998, it was Hu Jintao who announced China's reaction toward the bombing of the Chinese Embassy in Belgrade by American planes on behalf of the CCP Central Committee and the Chinese government. In November 2003, activity began in the Port of Dalian that did not stir up a lot of attention initially. The opening between the dry dock right next to pier number 4 where Varyag rested, and the jetty surrounding the whole port was being filled. November 2004 saw the completion of that filling work and various constructions were rising rigorously in that area. After these constructions were finished in March 2005, Varyag was taken to the dry dock in April. Therefore, it was made clear that all these fillings and constructions were made for Varyag. She was also painted grey in the four months within the dry dock, the colour of Chinese People's Liberation Army Navy.

These developments in China had ripples abroad, too. Because China had not acted discreetly. As previously mentioned, they did not even prevent idle photographers of the ship awaiting repair. The approach of those curious photographers was often ignored up until the edge of Varyag's island. The command center of the ship and flight operations had been obscured within the pier, but the situation changed with the need for a major modernization, and restoration. The taller buildings surrounding the port were raided, and photography was prevented.

Internationally, Taiwan was the first to draw attention to the work being done on Varyag in Dalian. On January 19, 2006, Taiwan's Ministry of National Defense (MND) published Port of Dalian-dwelling Varyag's satellite photos. A spokesperson of MND stated that "Varyag, previously claimed to be used as a touristic attraction point, would be used by China as a training ship," before adding completion of carrier war group would grant China the facilities for an attack on eastern Taiwan.

In October 2006, Lieutenant General Wang Zhiyuan, PLA's Vice-President of Department of General Armament Science and Technology Commission, made this explanation: "If we want to protect our interests on the oceans, we need to learn to produce aircraft carriers to develop our own carriers. We will not be able to form a real naval force consisting of carriers for another three or five years." This remark showed that Taiwan's concerns were not entirely baseless.

Taiwan's concerns paved the way for a significant change in the U.S. attitude towards the matter. It was previously mentioned that the U.S. Department of Defense (DOD), having shifted its focus mostly on Afghanistan and Middle East after 9/11 attacks, had not ever addressed Varyag in their reports about the military power of PRC until 2006. However, it is possible to find mentions of the carrier in reports dated 2006 and after.

2006 report referred to renovations of Varyag's deck, electrical workings, her hull having been painted with navy colour, and that China was interested in Su-33 naval fighter aircraft Russia produced for aircraft carriers; they also mentioned that PLA's ultimate purpose with Varyag remained unclear, but there were a series of possibilities. According to the report, these possibilities were: transforming Varyag into an operational aircraft carrier, a training or transition platform, or a floating theme park just as the original intention suggested.

2007 report repeated the possibilities in the previous year's report and further included predictions by analysts within and outside government that China could have an operational carrier until the end of the 12th Five Year Plan (2011-2015), but according to some other analysts, an operational aircraft carrier could be deployed in 2020 at the earliest.

DOD reports of 2008 and later would reveal Chinese intentions, lending credence to analysts who suggested the PRC could have their own carrier by the end of 2015. Here are relevant passages from those reports:

2008

There does not appear to be evidence that China has begun construction of an aircraft carrier. However, evidence in recent years increasingly suggests China's leaders may be moving forward with an aircraft carrier program.

Continued renovations to the former Soviet Kuznetsov-class aircraft carrier suggest China may choose to use the platform for training purposes. Moreover, the Russian press has reported Chinese interest in acquiring Russian Su-33 carrier-borne fighters. In October 2006, a Russian press report suggested early-stage negotiations were underway for China to purchase up to 50 such aircraft at a cost of $2.5 billion. However, there has been no announcement of a contract for the aircraft.

2009

China has an aircraft carrier research and design program, which includes continued renovations to the former Soviet Kuznetsov-class aircraft carrier Varyag.

China continues to show interest in procuring Su-33 carrier-borne fighters from Russia even though the ex-VARYAG aircraft carrier has yet to complete refurbishment at the Dalian shipyard.

The PLA Navy has reportedly decided to initiate a program to train 50 navy pilots to operate fixed-wing aircraft from an aircraft carrier. The program was reported to be four years long and would be followed by ship-borne training involving the ex-Varyag.

On the other hand, something of interest was happening in China which had not been in the DOD reports. In October 2009, an article titled "Mystery Is Revealed in Wuhan, and It Has a Flight Deck" on the military forum tiexue.net [Tiěxuè: lit. iron blood in Chinese] reported that a concrete replica of Varyag was being built in Wuhan. The city, whose name is known by virtually everyone in the world after the COVID-19 outbreak that started in 2019, harbored China Ship Research and Design Center, and the article stated that the aircraft carrier island and flight deck, getting built on top of a two-storey reinforced concrete office building, was almost identical in size to Varyag. Among some of the pictures from the article were a veiled plane and a helicopter on the deck, though it was unclear whether they were real or just models.

In fact, this structure was not the first concrete aircraft carrier China had built, built from their incredible frenzy for obtaining a carrier. PRC's first reinforced concrete carrier, Binzhou, was built within an artificial lake in the city of Binzou within Shandong province as a multi-functional leisure center and was in service in 2008. As of 2022, it would be impossible for the "carrier" – which is a simple replica of the oldest aircraft carrier still in service, USS Nimitz, at a cost of up to 19 million USD in total – to set sail on the world seas, and it was made to inevitably go bankrupt with its limited number of visitors and its casual management style. Indeed, it did go bankrupt.

However, Varyag's concrete replica should not be seen as the same type of "white elephant" as Binzhou. It would not be unfair to say that this structure, unfit for neither lift-offs nor landings, was instead designed for future aircraft carrier flights and deck crew to train for basic aircraft carrier operations.

2010

2010 report repeated opinions and findings of the two previous years. But one thing was added: It demonstrated that the state of Su-33 negotiations was not pleasant for China at all.

These negotiations reportedly stalled after Russia refused a request from China for an initial delivery of two trial aircraft. Russian defense ministry sources confirmed that the refusal was due to findings that China had produced its own copycat version of the Su-27SK fighter jet.

Having bought twenty-four Su-27 fighter jets from Russia in 1992, China further seized an opportunity arising from the Russian economic crisis of 1995. It bought the Su-27 technology, including its production line, and initiated a domestic version of the fighter jet under the name of J-11 in 1996. However, the fact that China developed an unlicensed version of Su-27 fighter jet without Russia's permission caused the bilateral relations to break down. Certainly, it was impossible for China to give up producing a fighter with features of taking off and landing in a short distance. Besides, it was not able to fold its wings or be used on aircraft carriers similar to Su-33. They could attempt to produce their own plane with reverse engineering based upon the unfinished Su-33 prototype they had bought from Ukraine in the early 2000s. And that's how it went.

2011

During the next decade China is likely to fulfill its carrier ambitions, becoming the last permanent member of the UN Security Council to obtain a carrier capability. In April 2011, China's Xinhua state news agency posted the newspaper's first pictures of the former Soviet carrier (Kuznetsov-class Hull-2) under renovation in Dalian, proclaiming that China will soon fulfill its "70-year aircraft carrier dreams."

Throughout 2010, the PRC continued refurbishing Kuznetsov Hull-2 (the ex-VARYAG), which China purchased from Ukraine in 1998. This carrier will likely begin sea trials in 2011, and the ship could become operationally available, although without aircraft, by the end of 2012. However, it will take several years for an operationally viable air group of fixed and rotary wing aircraft to achieve even a minimal level of combat capability. The PLA Navy has initiated a land-based program to begin training navy pilots to operate fixed-wing aircraft from an aircraft carrier. This program will probably be followed in about three years by fullscale ship-borne training aboard Kuznetsov Hull-2.

China has demonstrated an interest in foreign carrier-borne fighters and carrier aviation, but it appears that a domestic carrier aircraft production program is progressing. Currently in flight testing, the carrier aircraft, known as the J-15, is reportedly an unlicensed copy of a Russian Su-33, which China obtained from Ukraine in 2004.

In addition to the Kuznetsov-class carrier, the PLA Navy will likely build several additional carriers in Chinese shipyards. In March 2009, PLA Navy Admiral Wu Huayang affirmed, "China is capable of building aircraft carriers... Given the level of development in our country, I think we have such strength." Construction of China's first indigenous carrier, which would likely have a similar displacement and design of the Kuznetsov Hull-2, could begin as early as 2011. If China commences construction in 2011, the PLA Navy could have its first indigenous carrier achieving operational capability as early as 2015.

2012

China's aircraft carrier research and development program includes renovation of the Kuznetsov-class aircraft carrier Hull 2 (formerly the Varyag), which began sea trials in 2011. It will likely serve initially as a training and evaluation platform. Once China deploys aircraft capable of operating from a carrier, it should offer a limited capability for carrier-based air operations. Some components of China's first indigenously-produced carrier may already be under construction; that carrier could achieve operational capability after 2015. China likely will build multiple aircraft carriers and associated support ships over the next decade.

2013

The most significant development in the PLA Navy over the past year has been the sea trials and commissioning of China's first aircraft carrier, the Liaoning. The Liaoning was commissioned and entered service with the PLA Navy on September 25, 2012. The carrier most likely will conduct extensive local operations focusing on shipboard training, carrier aircraft integration, and carrier formation training before reaching an operational effectiveness in three to four years.

The J-15 aircraft conducted its first takeoffs and landings from the Liaoning on November 26, 2012. Subsequently, at least two aircraft conducted multiple landings and takeoffs from the ship.

Varyag began her first naval test on August 10, 2011. After completing her first four days of the test, the ship returned to Dalian. Before July 2012, she completed eight tests, then embarked on longer-running naval tests. After successfully completing a series of ten tests and taking the bow number "16" on September 3, 2012, Varyag was delivered to PLA at Port of Dalian on the morning of September 25 of that month, with a ceremony attended by top-level Chinese leaders including Head of State Hu Jintao and Prime Minister Wen Jiabao. She was then put into service. Everyone at that time thought that the ship would be named "Shi Lang", after the famous admiral who had conquered Taiwan during the Qing dynasty. However, the aircraft carrier was named "Liaoning" in honor of the province where she was renewed and restored. Senior Colonel Zhang Zheng was appointed as the first commander of the ship. After Liaoning came into service, China officially became the last country among U.N. Security Council permanent members to obtain an aircraft carrier.

Two months later Liaoning began to serve. During her cruise beginning on November 18 and lasting eight days, J-15 fighter planes – also known as "Flying Sharks" – made their first take-offs and landings (on November 23, despite the reported date). This proved an important milestone showing that China now had the ability to move planes to and from the carrier. Before long, the magnitude of this current achievement was only displayed on China's primary broadcasting organization, CCTV. In the footage, a descending J-15 fighter jet was shown catching the arresting wire on Liaoning's deck successfully before getting directed to a predetermined place for technical control, then the jet being prepared for flight and ascending from Liaoning's sloping launch platform under its own motor power. Cited with great pride by Chinese media, especially CCTV, this incident aroused great excitement in the country. Part of the footage went viral in no time. This video clip featured the launch of the fighter and the hand gestures of two deck crew, known as shooters, while they were letting the pilot know the launch was ready. This iconic scene, popularised by the movie Top Gun, had been regenerated twenty-six years later on Liaoning's deck, to the delight of Chinese people of all ages. Their expectation of "sixteen" was fulfilled, and Chinese people were making these gestures in all kinds of places, sharing their pictures online. Taking inspiration from the YouTube-famous song "Gangnam Style" by South Korean PSY, they called this new craze "Aircraft Carrier Style".

Even if things looked good for China, it was actually a bittersweet joy. Having felt unwell during the ship's return to Dalian and withdrawn to his quarters to rest after leaving the ship, Luo Yang, the chief engineer responsible for J-15 research and development, had a heart attack and passed away on the road to the hospital. After struggling for decades to develop the ability to deploy their fighter jets on the sea, China's success was dramatically clouded by Luo's death. The fact that the ministry of civil affairs declared Luo Yang a "martyr", since he made great contributions to the development of the country's first carrier-based fighter jet demonstrated the enormity of this loss.

AIRCRAFT CARRIER STYLE

2014

The most significant development in the PLA Navy over the past year has been the first long-range deployment and continued flight operations of China's first aircraft carrier, CV-16, the Liaoning. By September 2013, J-15s were conducting full-stops and takeoffs with weapon loads at full maximum gross weights. Additional full-stop landings, ramp takeoffs, and storage of aircraft in the hangar bay below the flight deck continued in October.

2015

In 2014, the PLA Navy's first aircraft carrier, Liaoning, returned to Dalian and conducted an extensive maintenance period, the first since entering service in September 2012. Following four months of maintenance, Liaoning returned to its homeport at Yuchi and continued flight integration training throughout 2014. The air wing is not expected to embark the carrier until 2015 or later. China also continues to pursue an indigenous aircraft carrier program and could build multiple aircraft carriers over the next 15 years.

2016

In 2015, the PLAN's first aircraft carrier, Liaoning, certified its first cohort of domestically trained J-15 operational pilots. The air wing is expected to deploy on the carrier in 2016. China also began construction of its first domestic aircraft carrier and could build multiple aircraft carriers over the next 15 years.

2017

In December 2016, the PLAN's first aircraft carrier, Liaoning, conducted its second-ever carrier task group integration training in the South China Sea. Even when fully operational, the Liaoning will not enable long-range power projection similar to U.S. Nimitz-class carriers. The Liaoning's smaller size limits the number of aircraft it can embark, while the ski-jump configuration limits restrict fuel and ordnance load.

VARYAG

2018

In 2017, the PLAN's first aircraft carrier, Liaoning, concluded its second training deployment to the South China Sea, its first with embarked J-15 fighter aircraft, and conducted its first port visit in Hong Kong. Though Liaoning has substantially less capability than a U.S. Navy carrier, it provides extended air defense coverage for at-sea task groups and is being used to develop further China's carrier pilots, deck crews, and tactics. In addition, China's first domestic aircraft carrier was launched in 2017 and will likely join the fleet by 2019. The new carrier is a modified version of Liaoning, but is similarly limited in its capabilities due to its lack of catapult and a smaller flight deck than U.S. carriers. However, China is expected to begin construction on its first catapult-capable carrier in 2018, which will enable additional fighter aircraft, fixed-wing early-warning aircraft, and more rapid flight operations.

As it is seen from DOD reports, the process was carried out just as China desired. Instead of learning to build an aircraft carrier from scratch, it would save quite a bit of time and money by learning to build a carrier based on Varyag. Indeed, that is what happened. The first domestic production aircraft carrier was built quickly and launched on April 26, 2017, with bow number "17". Named after yet another Chinese province, Shandong, the ship was largely mode led after Varyag (Liaoning). Although both Liaoning and Shandong have set sail to open seas, it is not quite possible to say that these are equivalent to those in the U.S. Navy. These carriers were using the STOBAR (Short Take-Off, Barrier-Arrested Recovery) system for fighters' take-offs and landings, and their not sole but most significant handicap was that they were designed to include a ski-jump take-off ramp, which enabled the fighters to make short distance take-offs. This meant the fighters would have to take off less frequently, with less fuel and ammunition load, and have a smaller fighting radius. Of course, it would not be realistic to think that China would confine itself to

AIRCRAFT CARRIER STYLE

STOBAR-style carriers. In their 2018 report, DOD estimated that China could start building a carrier the same year with the CATOBAR (Catapult Assisted Take-Off, Barrier Arrested Recovery) system, but this was a belated forecast. China had already silently begun building CATOBAR-style aircraft carriers in 2016, which were possessed only by the U.S. and France before.

Liaoning aircraft carrier arrives in Hong Kong. *Photo by Jerome Favre/EPA Images.*

Before long, the third carrier, named Fujian, with bow number "18" was launched on June 17, 2022, from Jiangnan Shipyard of Shanghai. Named after the south-eastern coastal province of Fujian, which has the Strait of Taiwan and Taiwan itself beyond it on its east, this ship was the first aircraft carrier domestically designed and built. Nevertheless, this time, China did not build only a CATOBAR-style aircraft carrier but also equipped the ship with an electromagnetic catapult instead of a traditional steam-powered catapult to improve its level of technology. This is how Fujian became the second aircraft carrier equipped with EMALS (Electromagnetic Aircraft Launch System) after the Ford-class aircraft carrier USS Gerald

R. Ford (CVN 78), which holds the title of the world's most outstanding aircraft carrier (as of 2022).

At this stage, there is only one indisputable answer to the inevitable question of "What next?": "Nuclear-fuelled aircraft carriers."

It would not be wrong to say that Varyag's long journey is akin to a movie with many actors. Undoubtedly, the first to mention among them is "businessman" Xu Zengping, by virtue of his roles both during the purchasing in Ukraine and afterward in China. It would be worth taking a look at what he has done after the journey was completed.

Having lapsed into a deep silence since 2002 as Varyag did, Xu settled with CASIL Clearing in 2007 regarding the case between them. According to this case, Xu Zengping had to pay 280 million Hong Kong dollars in installments. However, in a letter he wrote in 2008 to Hu Jintao, he claimed that actually, it was the state of China that owed him, that purchasing Varyag cost him a great deal, and his loss had reached 500 million USD. For compensation, he expressed himself like this: "Please give an order to the relevant public office. To pay by debt to more than one hundred creditors, I request 2 billion Hong Kong dollars in cash, and the remaining sum could be paid off suitably by negotiating with me."

As might be expected, his demand was refused, and Xu was not seen around for yet another long time. In fact, he was not even invited to the official service ceremony on September 25, 2012, two days after Varyag was handed over to PLAN, in which Varyag was renamed Liaoning. However, something unusual happened in 2013. On August 10, 2013, precisely one year after the re-equipped Varyag was put into service as Liaoning, Xu, and his family were received on the carrier by Captain Zhang Zheng. Apparently, Chinese authorities were not ignoring Xu altogether, though they steered clear of openly admitting his role in Varyag's purchase.

However, although long years have passed, Xu was determined to hold onto his claim for the government's debt to him. Such that, on March 28, 2016, the South China Morning Post newspaper published an interview with him titled "Chinese government still owes me US$120m for buying it an aircraft carrier, says PLA veteran". The content of the interview is as obvious as the title suggests. The credited journalist is none other than Minnie Chan, who had made most of the previous interviews with him.

Xu attempted to present himself as a patriot in the interview, saying, "If I had been out to profit from this, I would have sold the aircraft carrier once I'd bought it. But I didn't do that, did I?" However, his very next words clearly displayed his true intentions.

"It's really ridiculous that up until now, neither the central government nor the PLA has reimbursed me a single yuan. At least they should give me one official explanation – how come the carrier I bought was passed to the navy? And what was my role in the deal?"

When the past is scrutinized, it should not be too hard to see that Xu has not gotten the money he wanted from the government and is unlikely to get it in the future either.

Others, too, claimed China owed them money, even if the sums were not as hefty as Xu Zengping's claims for himself. Among them were Meral and Engin Aybay: Respectively, the wife and the son of the attorney Gunduz Aybay, who had managed the legal transactions for Varyag's passage through the straits but lost his life in late September 2001, about one month before the passage.

In 2004, the media shed light on a legal dispute involving the heirs of the late Gunduz Aybay. They claimed that they had not received a $40,000 attorney fee, prompting them to file a lawsuit against the Embassy of China in Ankara on behalf of China's Ministries of Finance, Defense, and Transportation. In the petition they presented to the court, they stated: "Regarding the matters of Varyag's pass through Turkey, Gunduz Aybay was appointed as the attorney. We would like the money taken from the defendants and given to ourselves, provided that our other rights from the contract would be reserved." Though they did not make any detailed explanations, according to certain sources, it is possible to say that the lawsuit concluded in favor of the Aybay family.

Another person who claimed China owed them money was Joop Timmermans, the boss of ITC, the Dutch ocean towage, salvage and heavy lift company that contracted the towage of Varyag.

This is what Timmermans said in the letter he wrote in January 2003 to China's Vice-Minister of Transportation and Minister of Naval Affairs:

"During the final delivery at Dalian, the tow was delayed, and under the agreed towing contract, demurrage is then due. We invoiced accordingly. However, the owners of the Varyag are refusing to pay this relatively small amount. (USD 30,000)

This is not only a money matter for ITC. It is also a moral matter.

I know your time is valuable, but I also hope you would be so kind as to give this matter some attention and hopefully you can find a solution to this relatively small problem."

However, it has never been possible for Joop Timmermans, a well-known, hugely respected person in salvage and towage businesses, and, in fact, who had been serving as the President of the ISU (International Salvage Union), to get his hands on this money.

APPENDIX

PHOTOGRAPHS

In this appendix, some of the rare and unpublished photographs of Varyag – from Joop Timmermans and Saim Oguzulgen's personal albums, along with unique photographs taken by Seyhun Agar, are presented.

PHOTOGRAPHS

Joop Timmermans' Album

Above and following two photos: Varyag under tow by the tugboat Suhaili in the Black Sea.

VARYAG

PHOTOGRAPHS

The tugboat Sandy Cape about to take over the tow from the tugboat Suhaili, which had an engine problem in the Black Sea.

Above and the following photo: Varyag under tow by the tugboat Sandy Cape in the Black Sea.

VARYAG

Some of the Sandy Cape's crew taking a walk on the flight deck of Varyag.

PHOTOGRAPHS

Three crew members of the tugboat Sandy Cape posing for a photo in front of the island of Varyag.

The crew returning to the tugboat Sandy Cape after visiting Varyag.

Saim Oguzulgen's Album

The invisible heroes of the Bosphorus – head maritime pilots, on the flybridge of Varyag just before the passage.

PHOTOGRAPHS

Pilot boat approaching Varyag so that Turkish experts can board the ship and inspect everything.

Inspection on the flight deck of Varyag.

VARYAG

Preliminary rehearsal of units participating in the towing operation.

The beginning of the towing operation.

PHOTOGRAPHS

Head maritime pilot Saim Oguzulgen directing the convoy's progress through the Bosphorus.

The convoy is heading towards the Bosphorus Bridge.

The convoy under the management of Saim Oguzulgen is progressing through the Dardanelles.

Saim Oguzulgen (1st from left) and Ruhan Cakiroglu (4th from left) with Chinese officials posing for the camera after visiting Varyag.

PHOTOGRAPHS

Seyhun Agar's Album

Above and following three photos: The unfinished ex-Soviet aircraft carrier Varyag under tow in Istanbul en route to China.

VARYAG

BIBLIOGRAPHY

"2011 Annual Report." China Aerospace International Holdings Limited. 2011. http://www.casil-group.com/download/eng/2011ar/e_31AR.pdf.

"Casino of Macau, China." Wayback Machine. April 21, 2006. https://web.archive.org/web/20060421192155/http://www.paul-andreu.com/pages/projets_recents_macao_gb.html.

Chan, Minnie. "Mission Impossible: How One Man Bought China Its First Aircraft Carrier." South China Morning Post. January 18, 2015. https://www.scmp.com/news/china/article/1681710/sea-trials-how-one-man-bought-china-its-aircraft-carrier.

Chan, Minnie. "Unlucky Guy Tasked with Buying China's Aircraft Carrier: Xu Zengping." South China Morning Post. April 29, 2015. https://www.scmp.com/news/china/diplomacy-defence/article/1779703/unlucky-guy-tasked-buying-chinas-aircraft-carrier-xu.

Chan, Minnie. "Chinese Government Still Owes Me US$120m for Buying It an Aircraft Carrier, Says PLA Veteran." South China Morning Post. March 27, 2016. https://www.scmp.com/news/china/diplomacy-defence/article/1931060/chinese-government-still-owes-me-us120m-buying-it.

Chou, Oliver. "Internet message spurs drive for aircraft carrier and status it will bring." South China Morning Post. June 14, 1999. https://www.scmp.com/article/285102/internet-message-spurs-drive-aircraft-carrier-and-status-it-will-bring.

"Clinton White House and Warships Sold to China." Newsmax. April 3, 2007. https://www.newsmax.com/pre-2008/clinton-white-house-and/2007/04/03/id/689465/.

Çağlayan, Suat. "MHP'li Bakan'ın Boğazlardan Geçirmek İstemediği O Uçak Gemisi Bakın Nereden Çıktı" [The aircraft carrier that the Minister does not want to pass through the Straits]. Oda TV. November 8, 2015. https://www.odatv4.com/yazarlar/prof-dr-suat-caglayan/mhpli-bakanin-bogazlardan-gecirmek-istemedigi-o-ucak-gemisi-bakin-nereden-cikti-84412.

Gertz, Bill. "Ukraine Won't Finish Russian Flattop." Washington Times. January 1, 1997.

"Independent Ukraine." Encyclopædia Britannica. n.d. https://www.britannica.com/place/Ukraine/Independent-Ukraine.

"Letter from Ambassador Prueher to Chinese Minister of Foreign Affairs Tang." The White House. April 11, 2001. https://georgewbush-whitehouse.archives.gov/news/releases/2001/04/20010411-1.html.

Li, Zhongxiao 李忠效. "辽宁舰前身瓦良格项目的二传手" [The Setter of the Predecessor of the Liaoning Ship Project, the Varyag Project]. China International News Media Group. November 29, 2018. http://cinm.hk/news.asp?id=4885&lb=22.

Lintner, Bertil. Blood Brothers: Crime, Business and Politics in Asia. 1st ed. Allen and Unwin, 2002.

Luck, Adam, and Raymond Ma. "Beijing Calms Waters for Floating Casino." South China Morning Post. September 9, 2001. https://www.scmp.com/article/357180/beijing-calms-waters-floating-casino.

"Macao Gaming History." Gaming Inspection and Coordination Bureau. n.d. https://www.dicj.gov.mo/web/en/history/index.html.

Morrison, Micah. "The Macau Connection." The Wall Street Journal. February 26, 1998. https://www.wsj.com/articles/SB888439204883313500.

"Ng Lap Seng, O EmpresáRio Tóxico Que Jacobs Quis Evitar" [Ng Lap Seng, the toxic businessman that Jacobs wanted to avoid]. Ponto Final. October 12, 2015. https://pontofinalmacau.wordpress.com/2015/10/12/ng-lap-seng-o-empresario-toxico-que-jacobs-quis-evitar/.

Storey, Ian, and You Ji. "China's Aircraft Carrier Ambitions." Naval War College Review 57, no. 1 (2004).

Xiang, Ruicheng 向瑞成. "中国辽宁舰前身瓦良格号航母不是徐增平先生购买的" [The predecessor of the Chinese Liaoning Ship, the Varyag aircraft carrier, was not purchased by Mr. Xu Zengping]. China International News Media Group. September 30, 2016. http://cinm.hk/news.asp?id=536&lb=22.

Xiang, Ruicheng 向瑞成. "让证据说话：瓦良格号航母是戴岳和张勇购买的" [Let the evidence speak: The aircraft carrier Varyag was purchased by Dai Yue and Zhang Yong]. China International News Media Group. November 1, 2016. http://cinm.hk/news.asp?id=587&lb=22.

Xiang, Ruicheng 向瑞成. "让法律说话：揭开东方汇中购买瓦良格号航母神秘面纱" [Let the Law Speak: Unveiling the Mystery of Dongfang Huizhong's Purchase of the Varyag Aircraft Carrier]. China International News Media Group. January 17, 2017. http://cinm.hk/news.asp?id=686&lb=22.

Ye, Biao 叶飙. "慢船来中国瓦良格号来华过程揭秘" [The Secrets of Varyag's Journey to China]. Southern Weekly. April 4, 2013.

ACKNOWLEDGMENTS

Firstly, I would like to thank the visitors from all around the world who followed my website "varyagworld.com", where I shared photos, news and mysteries regarding Varyag since the first day I began to research the subject, and made me stick to my research; and innumerable people who shared their information outright. And I would like to specifically mention the names of people who made invaluable contributions to this work.

Ramazan Mirzaoglu, then state minister of maritime affairs, who, with his modest personality and well-spoken oratory, narrated his stance during Varyag's passage through Turkish Straits;

Ruhan Cakiroglu, then Istanbul district manager of the undersecretariat of maritime affairs, who told of those days as clearly as if it was yesterday, who changed my perspective, and brought new horizons for my work;

Head Maritime Pilot Saim Oguzulgen, the consummate mariner, who, with his idiosyncratically vibrant and gripping narration, explained the Turkish Straits and the operation of Varyag's towage through them, and has been kind enough to read the manuscript and who wished to contribute with his precious criticism;

Joop Timmermans, who generously opened his Varyag archives and shared his knowledge with me;

Mehmet Sait Guven, my editor, who touched my sentences with his heart;

Tuna Erdogdu, from kitapeditoru.com, who steered me with his vision in the world of authorship, where I happen to be a stranger;

Mert Dogruer, who meticulously translated the book into English, and Graham Sheard, the English language editor;

Aysel Demirayak, my mother, who provided her full support from my earliest idea;

Nilgun Yucel Demirayak, my lovely wife, who is always with me and never lets me fall into despair;

Hande Demirayak, my dear daughter, who contributed with her youthful ideas and perspective;

Thank you all for your contributions, suggestions, support, criticism, and, most importantly, your faith in this. Without you, this book may never have been written.

ABOUT THE AUTHOR

Ahmet Hikmet Demirayak has completed BSc in Environmental Engineering at Middle East Technical University. The university improved him as a computer programmer, while bringing him the skills of researching. From the 1980s, when he first transferred a computer programme he wrote on a paper to the main computer by using a punch card machine. He has written hundreds of computer programmes consisting of thousands of lines, and has also worked as a software analyst. He thinks writing a book is quite different and definitely a much more challenging experience than writing a computer programme.

Made in the USA
Coppell, TX
31 March 2024

30755801R00095